Chemically Dependent Older Adults
How Do We Treat Them?

About the authors:

Mundie Merrill has fifteen years' experience in the chemical dependency field and presently works at the Libertas Chemical Dependency Rehabilitation Program, Springfield, Illinois.

Fr. Philip Graham Kraft, M.H.S., S.C.A.C., is an ordained Catholic priest and a chemical dependency program planner for the State of Illinois.

Margaret Gordon is a staff nurse who works with older adults at Riverside Medical Center, Minneapolis, Minnesota.

Mary Marrs Holmes, L.S.W., has nine years experience in the chemical dependency field and four years working directly with older adults. She conducts workshops and training about chemical dependency and older adults.

Bobbie Walker has worked with chemically dependent older adults for twelve years. She has a private outpatient program in Edina, Minnesota and has authored *Caring and Coping: For Family Members of Older Adults in Recovery* and coauthored with Phil Kelly *The Elderly: A Guide for Counselors*, both published by Hazelden Educational Materials.

Photo credits: Mike Yencho—Cover, Chapter One (before
                  page 1), and Chapter Five
                  (page 100)

          John Keskinen—Chapter Two (page 14),
                  Chapter Three (page 38),
                  and Chapter Four (page 68)

Chemically Dependent Older Adults

How Do We Treat Them?

Merrill, Kraft, Gordon, Holmes & Walker

With a Foreword by
Daniel J. Anderson, Ph. D

 HAZELDEN®

First published April 1990.

ISBN: 0-89486-603-6
Library of Congress Catalog Card Number: 89-81621

Printed in the United States of America.

Editor's note:
  Hazelden Educational Materials offers a variety of information on chemical dependency and related areas. Our publica-
tions do not necessarily represent Hazelden or its programs,
nor do they officially speak for any Twelve Step organization.
  The stories in this book are true. Names and some details
have been changed to protect people's anonymity.

CONTENTS

FOREWORD

It is now common knowledge that more people over age sixty-five are alive today than ever before in the history of this country. By the year 2000, nearly 20 percent of our population will be age sixty-five or older, double the present estimate of 11 percent.

Obviously, we must plan now to meet the many needs of this fastest growing age group in the United States. Unfortunately, our perceptions of aging tend to be somewhat ambivalent and ambiguous. We overlook or overstate either the happy side or the sad side of the aging process, frequently not attending to the fact that aging involves both happiness and sadness, and more. The great value of this book is that it deals with the problems of aging with full awareness of both the happy and the sad side, and more.

The need for this book may be stated in a straightforward fashion: It deals with practical and tested strategies to help our aging population recover from chemical dependency problems. Each contributor is an experienced clinician who writes out of her or his own experience in successfully helping older adults to recover from a variety of chemical dependency problems.

It is from this experience that the authors are able to offer practical advice and wisdom while at the same time being fully aware that chemically dependent older adults defy description as a homogeneous group. Thus, each author is acutely aware that each older adult represents a unique composition or integration of the happy and the sad side of aging in terms of physical and emotional health, family background, vocational and avocational interests, socio-cultural influences, and a wide range of life experiences.

Not only do the authors demonstrate their respect and understanding for the individuality of each chemically dependent older adult, but they also seem to have a special understanding of the unique needs chemically dependent older adults have throughout the whole continuum of chemical dependency treatment. Thus, in a sense, this book reads like a highly well-thought-out bill of rights for older adults who may become chemically dependent. By way of example, each chapter in turn clearly demonstrates that older people, along with people in all age groups, have the following rights.

- To have their chemical dependency appropriately intervened with and assessed.
- To be referred to an appropriate treatment program that will address their special physical, psychological, social, and spiritual needs.
- To receive aftercare services that address their specific needs following treatment.

Still another chapter deals specifically with the families of older adults who have chemical dependency problems. Here, as in every other chapter, there is acute sensitivity to not only the needs of these significant others, but also to the contributions that they can make in aiding the recovery of the chemically dependent older adult.

Because this book makes very specific recommendations for intervention, treatment, and aftercare, it might seem to be addressed primarily to a professional audience. However, the level of communication, the practical and sensible recommendations, I think, make this book suitable for any friend, relative, or caregiver of an older adult who has a chemical dependency problem.

I think it is important to point out that this is a book of hope, based on long-term clinical experience in working with older adults with chemical dependency problems. The authors know from their own experience that older adults with such problems can make excellent recoveries from their chemical dependency. They are well aware that, despite the apparent complexity, the simultaneous treatment of chemical dependency and other concurrent illnesses in older adults is not only cost-effective but health-enhancing. In this sense, it is very helpful for all of us to learn that older adults with chemical dependency problems can recover even though they do have some unique and special needs that must be addressed.

In summary, this book is a gold mine of practical strategies and techniques that address the unique problems of the older person with chemical dependency problems.

DANIEL J. ANDERSON
President Emeritus
Hazelden Foundation

At fifteen, I applied myself to the study of wisdom;
at thirty I grew stronger in it;
at forty I no longer had doubts;
at sixty there was nothing on earth that could shake me;
at seventy I could follow the dictates of my heart
without disobeying the moral law.
                                        – Confucius

CHAPTER ONE

INTERVENTION

Mundie Merrill

The Process of Intervention

Intervention is a process friends and relatives use to confront a chemically dependent person with the truth about his or her chemical abuse. There are basic steps that the usual intervention model follows, but each intervention is also unique, depending on the abuser and the circumstances surrounding his or her abuse. This chapter is about adapting the usual intervention model to meet the special needs of intervening in an older adult's chemical abuse.

Intervention usually begins with a concerned person contacting a counselor at a treatment facility or mental health agency about a friend or loved one's chemical abuse. He or she usually wants to know how to approach the chemical abuser, what to say, and how to ask the person to get help. After a screening interview with the concerned person to determine if chemical abuse is the problem, the counselor may ask if other people are similarly concerned about the person's chemical

1

abuse. Some of these people may eventually become members of the intervention team.

There are special problems with intervening in an older adult's chemical abuse, the first of which is forming an intervention team. One problem is that there are often few, if any, people left in the older adult's immediate family to contact as potential intervention team members. Some family members may have died; others may be seriously ill or disabled. If the older adult has children, they may be more concerned about the dependent parent's spouse, if he or she is alive, than they are about the dependent parent.

How Children of the Chemically Dependent Older Adult May Respond

Children may have given up on trying to help the dependent parent. Also, children may not be able to take time away from their jobs, their own families, or be able or willing to contribute the money that may be necessary to help their parent pay for treatment. Children of chemically dependent older adults are in the middle, feeling the stress of caring for their young families, but also of having to care for their older loved ones. When forced to choose, they may be unwilling to give more time or energy to their dependent parent.

Children may also be unable to help with an intervention if they live far away from their parent. Or, they may simply choose not to participate. They may have cut themselves off emotionally from their parents because of pain they felt early in life due to a parent's chemical abuse. Also, it is not unusual to find that children have attitudes that prevent them from taking action to help their parent. They may view chemical dependency in old age as an incurable condition, believing there is no hope for change. They may even excuse or justify their parent's behavior by saying he or she has a "right" to enjoy a few drinks in old age. They may say their parent worked hard, raised a family, and is now entitled to a few happy times. In

2

other words, children may not view their parent's chemical abuse as harmful.

It is important to keep in mind that control over family money may also be an issue. The thinking may be, Why invest money in treatment when one is old and doesn't have much longer to live? And if the older adult is living with his or her children, alcohol and other chemical abuse may be ignored, even encouraged by the family. In some families, the older adults may be viewed as a burden or a nuisance; their chemical abuse keeps them from interfering with the family, keeps them out of the way and quiet.

Involving the Spouse

Involving the spouse of the chemically dependent older person in an intervention raises additional issues. The spouse may feel fearful due to the exposure of chemical dependency in the family – fear of his or her spouse having to retire early or getting fired as a result of treatment. The spouse may also fear financial difficulty and that their present standard of living may no longer be possible. Fear of having to work outside the home may be an issue for women who have worked in the home all their life. To the spouse of the chemically dependent older adult, confronting the chemical dependency may threaten their retirement dreams – a second home in another part of the country, travel to places never before visited.

There are also other personal losses partners may feel when contemplating the consequences of treatment for their spouse. They may fear the loss of companionship and the rearrangement of family responsibilities. For example, if during the marriage the woman had little responsibility for family finances, a consequence of treatment may be that she has to learn how to deal with all of these concerns. Conversely, if during the marriage the man had little to do with taking care of social events, cooking, cleaning, and washing clothes, he will have to learn to do these things as a result of his spouse enter-

3

ing treatment. These changes may be difficult to accept for the dependent person and heavy to carry for the spouse.

In addition to the family issues that make forming an effective intervention team difficult, there are other issues such as the fact that the chemically dependent older person may no longer live in his or her old neighborhood. Consequently, long-time friends and neighbors may not be near to help with an intervention. The older adult's new residence may be a high-rise where he or she has made few, if any, new friends. And, like anyone else, the older adult feels a painful loss due to these changes, and may have difficulty adjusting to the new and strange environment. It is common for a person to become depressed and isolated when faced with these losses and this often masks chemical abuse.

OVERCOMING BARRIERS TO FORMING AN INTERVENTION TEAM

Potential Intervention Team Members

After approaching an assessment counselor about an older person's chemical abuse, it is important for the concerned person and the counselor to think creatively about who could be a part of an intervention team. Who else might be concerned about the older person's chemical abuse? Maybe the delivery man who brings several bottles of liquor to the person's apartment each week, or the local pharmacist who notices disturbing changes in the older person's appearance would be willing to become intervention team members. Tenants in the person's apartment complex, or neighbors across the street, may have information that indicates the need for treatment. They may have seen cigarette burns on the older person's skin, furniture, or clothing; smelled alcohol on the person's breath; noticed an unsteady gait, poor personal hygiene, poor memory, confusion, bruises, broken bones, accidents, or falls that indicate chemical abuse and the need for treatment.

Other possible team members, such as health care providers, repeatedly observe signs of chemical dependency in older adults and may be key participants in an intervention. Physicians, emergency room attendants, nurses, or pharmacists may have noticed signs of chemical abuse but assumed they were signs of old age. When an older person uses emergency room services, they, and sometimes their family, take care to disguise chemical abuse. An emergency room visit is often attributed to a fall caused by poor eyesight, poor coordination, poor balance due to inner ear problems, or any number of other things except chemical abuse. Emergency room records and personnel can make an important contribution to the intervention team. Similarly, other medical records and the observations of a physician may indicate chemical abuse that other participants were unaware of.

Mental health workers providing counseling services to older adults are another possible source of information. Their diagnosis of depression due to loss of family, home, job, role, and status in the community may mask chemical abuse in an older adult. When an older adult complains of having trouble falling asleep or of having no appetite, the therapist may prescribe antidepressant medications that can compound the problem of chemical abuse. Knowledge of this can make for a more successful intervention.

Since many older adults are retired, intervention team members cannot usually be drawn from the workplace. When a younger person has a chemical abuse problem, the workplace is more important. Their jobs offer them status in the community, purpose, income, and are important to their overall survival. And while some older adults continue to gain status, purpose, and income from their jobs, many are retired. If they do work, their job is probably part-time and comes with different expectations than full-time employment. When problems occur at work, older workers are often excused because of poor health, lack of transportation, or poor weather conditions. Yet, contacting a part-time employer can yield important information, so it should not be discouraged.

THE ASSESSMENT INTERVIEW

The first meeting of the intervention team's prospective members is called the assessment interview. Here, prospective team members document specific indications of the older adult's chemical dependency. The intervention counselor guides this process by asking pointed questions of the team members such as:

- Do you overlook the dependent person's behavior, believing it is just a reaction to medication, a normal symptom of old age, or that the older person has a "right" to enjoy a few drinks in his or her old age?
- Do you become embarrassed at the dependent person's drug related behavior?
- Do you deny his or her drug abuse by ignoring or rationalizing it?
- Have you taken over roles the dependent person used to have in the family?
- Have you increased your alcohol or other drug use?
- Have you noticed symptoms of stress in yourself such as nausea, ulcers, sweating palms, or bitten fingernails?
- Do you feel that, as a child, relative, or friend that you should do more but don't want to?

These questions help prospective team members understand more clearly that what they are seeing and feeling is a result of chemical dependency. At this session, prospective team members begin to understand what enabling behaviors are and how they, as family members or friends, have responded to the older person's chemical dependency. It is important for family members to reduce their guilt and shame

6

about chemical dependency, and to understand that this disease is no one's fault. Reducing guilt and shame in family members of a chemically dependent older adult may require more effort than in other families because the secret of chemical dependence may have been kept for thirty years or more. Confronting their guilt and shame will cause family members to come to some realizations about their life, as well as the life of their parent or partner. These realizations include

• recognizing the loss of a healthy childhood.
• remembering trauma.
• admitting resentments against both parents.
• recognizing the loss of self-esteem.
• acknowledging compulsive behaviors in themselves.
• recognizing an inability to trust.
• becoming aware of their own parenting behaviors.

Family members will need time and help to understand some of those feelings.

THE INTERVENTION TEAM

After the assessment interview, the intervention team is chosen. Those with firsthand knowledge of the older adult's chemical abuse, changes in his or her attitudes, behaviors, and expression of feelings, are the desired team members. The intervention counselor needs to make it clear to team members that they need to have a definite commitment to the task. They should be asked to write their concerns about how their relationship will change with the chemically dependent older adult as a result of their participation in the intervention. And they should discuss these concerns. It should also be made clear to team members that they will be expected to attend all inter-

7

vention team meetings, including the

- preintervention meeting.
- confrontation meeting with the chemical abuser.
- post-intervention meeting.
- follow-up meetings regarding treatment recommendations given by the counselor.

The first task of the intervention team is to write the statement that will be used to confront the older adult. This statement should be worded so that it is respectful and clear, not condescending. It should include the consensus of the group, be carefully constructed, and be able to be said by each team member from memory. The purpose of the statement is to inform the chemically dependent older adult that the team is receiving counseling and that he or she will be asked to participate at the appropriate time. There will be no element of surprise to the chemical abuser.

There are several parts of the intervention process, including three two-hour family sessions weekly. Through lectures, films, and role-play, the team will learn more about the disease of chemical dependency, enabling behaviors, and the need for their own recovery. The team will also learn how, when the intervention occurs, to relay their information in a caring, compassionate, and receptive way to the dependent person.

The team also needs to develop a *What If* strategy. What if the older adult refuses to enter treatment? What will this mean for the team members? The What If strategy is often called the *New Rule* strategy. It states that if the abuser rejects the need for treatment, the team members will no longer be a part of the enabling system for the chemical abuser. They will form a recovery plan of their own. There will be no covering up for the dependent person's actions. Each team member decides to be free to enjoy and grow in their recovery, and to be as free as possible from the impact of chemical dependency on them. These are not threats to the dependent person, but statements of what will happen if he or she refuses treatment.

Dress Rehearsal

The next step of the process is the preintervention meeting or *dress rehearsal*. At this point, team members will need the conviction and courage to say what they actually saw. At this stage, the team will begin to research treatment alternatives for the older adult. Because of the unique needs of older adults, finding an appropriate treatment facility may take more time and research than it would for a younger person. Many treatment facilities are simply not geared for older adult patients. The programs at many treatment centers are conducted at a pace that is too fast for older adults, especially those who are cognitively impaired. Other treatment centers may choose not to admit older adult patients because of their belief that an older adult's chance for recovery is slim. Some treatment staff even believe there is little motivation for an older person to recover.

The factors that work together to make treatment successful for younger people are not always present in older adults. Younger patients have usually used chemicals for fewer years, have more support systems in their community, fewer health concerns, and friends who are emotionally connected to them. Older adult patients, however, often have major losses associated with aging, and often lack a viable support system. It is true, some motivation for recovery is indeed absent. Consequently, finding an appropriate treatment center, one sympathetic to the needs of older adult abusers, is crucial for treatment to be effective.

Aftercare Planning by the Intervention Team

The final issue to be addressed by the intervention team is aftercare planning. If the older person does well in treatment, what can be done after treatment to ensure continued recovery? The older person may not be welcome in his or her former residence because of inappropriate behavior when using chemicals. And nursing homes sometimes deny admission to the chemically dependent. Also, the older person may have difficulty attending aftercare groups due to lack of transportation and fear of going out after dark. It is important for the team to have several aftercare options to pursue, depending on how the older adult responds to treatment. Specific details to consider for aftercare planning are included in this book's section on aftercare.

Once a treatment facility is chosen, the team needs to refine the information they will present to the chemical abuser, and they need to review the New Rules for a final time. By now, all the necessary planning should be completed. As a final precaution, the team may choose to brainstorm about any potential roadblocks. It is important to consider the following questions:

- Will the chemical abuser enter treatment immediately following the confrontation session?
- Is there a bed immediately available at the chosen treatment center?
- Is there anything that needs to be done about the person's health insurance?
- If there is still an employer, how should they be notified?

These and other practical preparations must be made *before* the intervention confrontation session. Much of the success of an intervention lies in meticulous planning and careful execution of the team plan. The role of the counselor is intended to be one of teacher and coach. For the confrontation meeting, the counselor may often ask another counselor to join the meeting as a co-counselor. It is possible that the counselor, in his or her teaching and interaction with the family, has become emotionally involved and thus becomes part of the family system. Another staff person can bring balance to the team. Once the team is confident it can do the task, the date and time for the confrontation session with the chemical abuser can be set.

INTERVENTION BEGINS

The confrontation session with an older adult chemical abuser needs to be conducted in a quiet place that is easily accessible to the person. Older people sometimes have limited mobility and are usually accustomed to a quiet lifestyle. Possible sites include a doctor's office, a conference room in the emergency room area of a hospital, an office in a local senior center, the home of the older person, or any other place that seems appropriate for a private counseling session.

At the confrontation session, the chemical abuser is confronted with the feelings of family and friends, and the facts of his or her chemical abuse. After each team member expresses his or her feelings and describes what he or she has seen of the older adult's chemical abuse, the person is asked to enter treatment. Obviously, two outcomes are possible: the person enters treatment as hoped or the person refuses. Each member of the team needs to be firm in following his or her personal plan of recovery regardless of the older adult's decision. Whatever the outcome of the intervention, the family needs to be encouraged to view the intervention as part of a process, not as an isolated event at which failure or success is determined.

An Illustration of a Successful Older Adult Intervention

Joe and Dora's Story

> Joe, a retired executive, visited a counselor. He told the therapist his story. A few months earlier, he had retired, and he and Dora, his wife, were anticipating many happy retirement years. But Joe soon realized that this was not going to happen because of Dora's chemical abuse. In her delusional condition, Dora was convinced that she was due to die from muscular dystrophy. Joe suspected this was not true because Dora

11

had never had any health problems. Joe noticed, however, that Dora's chemical abuse had steadily increased over the past few years, and he suspected she might be chemically dependent.

Dora walked with a staggering gait, had dramatic personality shifts where she became irritable and verbally abusive to loved ones. Dora also had become isolated and withdrawn, yet Joe said she had once been an extroverted and articulate person. Joe shared his observations and concerns with a physician and was referred to the local hospital-based chemical dependency treatment center to talk with a chemical dependency counselor.

After spending some time with the chemical dependency counselor, Joe and the counselor were able to develop an intervention strategy, and the two began work on forming an intervention team. The team was eventually composed of two of Dora's grown children and four couples from their bridge club. Training and rehearsal began. On the day of the intervention, Dora, in her wheelchair, moved from person to person venting her anger. After the hour-long session, she still denied dependency but agreed to treatment. It was successful. Today, Joe and Dora are enjoying their retirement years, much as they had originally intended.

In summary, using intervention with chemically dependent older adults requires the counselor and the intervention team to be creative, sensitive, and open to new concepts. It is not true that the chemical abuser must hit bottom in order to be receptive to treatment. Chemical dependency *is* a terminal disease. It not only takes the life of the chemical abuser, but affects family members and friends as well. Older adults have the right to a life free of chemicals. Intervening in an older adult's chemical abuse can help restore an enjoyable life to the older adult and his or her family. By responding to the chemically dependent older adult with love and concern, and by inviting him or her to enter treatment, the team is helping the person make the choice to live.

To know how to grow old
is the master work of wisdom, and one of the most difficult
chapters in the great art of living.
                                        — Henri Frédéric Amiel

CHAPTER TWO

ASSESSMENT

Fr. Philip Graham Kraft, M.H.S., S.C.A.C

You are a chemical dependency professional. A sixty-eight-year-old woman comes into your office and you observe that she has an unsteady gait and hand tremors. She is debilitated, confused, and disoriented. Her ability for recent memory recall is impaired, and she is unable to clearly state where she is and why she is appearing before you. Can you attribute her condition to aging, drinking, drugging, or a combination of these factors?

When a chemical dependency assessment counselor is faced with these symptoms in a forty-eight-year-old person, the counselor would aptly assess them as indicators of either chemical dependency or mental illness. But, when faced with these symptoms in an older person, the assessment counselor, like other health care professionals who usually are not aware of the special concerns and needs of older adults, is likely to attribute these symptoms to aging rather than chemical dependency.

AN ASSESSMENT OVERVIEW

Sorting Through the Labels

Accurate assessment is sometimes hampered by the blurry dividing lines between labels such as: alcoholism, alcohol abuse, alcohol problems, chemical dependency, substance abuse, drug dependency, addiction, aged, elderly, and old. The Social Security Administration describes age categories in the following manner:

- *old* as age 55 - 64
- *elderly* as age 65 - 74
- *aged* as age 75 - 84
- *very old* as age 85 and over

Senior citizens? Older citizens? Aged? Elderly? As one sixty-three-year-old man said, "I'm not elderly, I'm older." Each of these labels has its supporters and detractors, and those who study aging are in a quandary as to which labels accurately reflect each person's aging condition.

The terms referring to chemical dependency and aging elicit emotional reactions often charged with feelings of shame, sinfulness, weakness, and loss of control. For example, to label my mother "addicted" is, for her, to be emotionally assigned to the criminal element. To label my father "alcoholic" means, to him, that he belongs to a weak-willed, sinful element. Similarly, to label a person "elderly" may be, for him or her, an assignment to a life of pain and loss lived in a nursing home. One seventy-year-old gentleman who reviewed the living quarters of a sheltered care facility for senior citizens said, " The place is full of old people; I'm going back home."

Customizing Assessment Tools

Chemical dependency assessment tools have been revised over the years because they were often not sensitive to cultural, gender, and age factors. American Indians, African-Americans, women, and adolescents often did not fit the model of working, middle-class males on whom most assessment tools were based.

Age is now also recognized as a factor to be considered in the assessment of chemical dependency. For example, there has been in recent years the rapid development of a separate treatment track for adolescents. Recognizing the need for assessment tools that are sensitive to chemically dependent older people is part of this evolution of singling out the unique needs of various populations.

Today, the most frequently used assessment tools rely on the frequency and quantity of drug use, and on occupational, social, legal, familial, health, and spiritual problems to diagnose chemical dependency. In the following chapter, I will discuss first why standard assessment tools do not always work for older adults, and I will follow with a suggested assessment procedure specific to the needs of older adults. In addition to a chemical dependency assessment, I will also suggest that older persons be assessed for their physical ability to handle the activities of daily living (ADL).

Older chemically dependent people are categorized into two groups: *early-onset* alcoholics – those who have been abusing alcohol or other drugs excessively for many years. And *late-onset* alcoholics – those whose dependency is fairly recent, perhaps as a response to loss or illness. Of older adult chemically dependent people, two-thirds are early-onset and one-third are late-onset.[1]

---

[1] S. Zimberg, "Diagnosis and Management of the Elderly Alcoholic," in *Alcohol & Drug Abuse in Old Age*, R. M. Atkinson, ed. (Washington D.C.: American Psychiatric Press, 1984), 26.

Assessing Frequency and Quantity of Use

Standard models used to measure the frequency and quantity of alcohol and other drug consumption in chemically dependent people are not as applicable to older adults as they are to younger adults. An older person's ability to metabolize alcohol and other drugs is slower than that of younger and middle-aged adults. This is due to changes in body weight, distribution of fatty tissue, and a decrease in renal function and excretion, all of which are a normal part of the aging process. Older people may use alcohol or other drugs in lesser amounts than younger people, and, in many cases, in lesser amounts than they used in their younger days, and still experience greater effects of the drug due to these physical changes.

As with alcohol and other drugs, the accuracy of the frequency and quantity norm as applied to prescription and nonprescription medications is also affected by the aging process and the slowed metabolic rate of older adults. This results in diminished tolerance, which, when added to the fact that older people consume more prescription and nonprescription medications than the rest of the population, makes it difficult to distinguish between the use and misuse of these medications.

Baum and his associates reported in 1985 that the mean number of prescriptions per year increases with age.[2]

- Those under age 45 received 4.6 prescriptions per year
- Those age 45 - 54 received 6.9 prescriptions per year
- Those age 55 - 64 received 9.3 prescriptions per year
- Those age 65 - 74 received 13.6 prescriptions per year
- Those age 75 and over received 16.9 prescriptions per year

---

[2] C. Baum, D. L. Kennedy, and M. D. Forbes, "Drug Utilization in the Geriatric Age Group," in *Geriatric Drug Use: Clinical & Social Perspectives*, S. R. Moore and T. W. Teal, eds. (Elmsford, N.Y.: Pergamon Books, 1985), 65.

Over-the-counter drugs frequently contain ingredients such as alcohol or caffeine to assure that the consumer feels an effect. One cough medicine, which this author knows was the favorite of grade-school children in the early 1970s, contains 25 percent alcohol and comes with its own shot (dosage) cup.

Assessing Occupational Problems

Exploring occupational problems is not likely to be as helpful in assessing chemical dependency in older adults as it is in assessing younger adults. Older adults are more likely to be retired. Their previous employer may have confused chemical dependency with aging and carried them on the payroll until retirement, unaware of the chemical dependency problem. Or, the employer may have noticed the older person's impaired performance, but rather than confront the illness, they may have instead decided that he or she has contributed years of service and should be "rewarded" with early retirement.

Other obstacles in obtaining work-related information to assess a retired individual include the retirement or death of supervisors and co-workers. Or, some employers may no longer be in business. Also, compared to younger women, many older women have not worked outside the home, or have worked in part-time positions where their behavior is less likely to be monitored closely.

Assessing Social Problems

Older people may have undergone changes in their social lives that isolate them in their drug abuse, and that make it more difficult for their dependency to be discovered by family, friends, or service providers. For example, they or their friends may be ill and unable to socialize as they used to. Geographical distance between older people and their family and friends can also hinder awareness of a drug problem. And service providers to older adults may not spot a problem, since becoming less socially active is often viewed by society and health care professionals as a natural result of aging, not a result of chemical dependency.

Assessing Legal Problems

Chemically dependent older adults often isolate themselves in their homes, so their dependency is less likely to come to the attention of law enforcement agencies. These are some other reasons why an older adult's chemical dependency is rarely brought to the attention of the police.

- People over sixty-five make up a very small percentage of those arrested for drunk and drugged driving. Although driving under the influence of prescription drugs is a growing concern, it is difficult to prove in court.
- Spouses are unlikely to report physical or verbal abuse to the police because they may have lived with their mate for so long that they are reluctant to place their spouse in trouble or bring shame on the family.
- The family may simply lack the financial, physical, and emotional resources to involve their chemically dependent older person with law enforcement officials in any way.
- In the case of late-onset chemical dependency, family and friends often attribute an older adult's disruptive actions to aging rather than to chemical dependency.

Apart from directly involving law enforcement in an older person's drug use, another legal issue unique to chemically dependent older adults is the concern of guardianship or power of attorney due to the person's inability to care for themselves or their finances. This may need to be discussed during an older adult assessment.

20

Assessing Family Problems

In assessing the family problems of an early-onset older adult alcoholic, counselors often find that problems are so long-standing that the person may have been abusing chemicals for most of his or her adult life and that the family no longer cares what happens to the older person. An emotional attachment may not exist.

Other family members may also be chemically dependent. In fact, the chemically dependent family members – especially if they feel their own chemical use is threatened – may drink or abuse other drugs with the older adult. These family members may try to rationalize the dependent person's abuse of chemicals, withdraw the older person from the care of chemical dependency professionals, or place the older person in a nursing home where the dependency will not be addressed.

On the other hand, family problems of the late-onset alcoholic are more often recent problems – just as the dependency is recent. But because chemically dependent older adults no longer have children living at home with them, family members may have little firsthand information that implicates chemical dependency as the cause of family problems. The following are problems the family of a late-onset chemically dependent person may have in confronting the dependency.

- They often believe prescribed medications are "safe" and may find it difficult to attribute misuse of these as a factor in the distress of the family.
- The children may overlook their parent's chemical abuse because during the years they were in the home there were no problems with the abuse of medications and alcohol.
- The family of the late-onset chemically dependent person

is more likely to believe aging is the cause of distress than alcohol or medication abuse.

Assessing Health Problems

Chronic health problems are not usually a factor in the assessment of a younger adult, but should always be considered when assessing an older adult for chemical dependency. Health problems in older persons, such as arthritis, stroke, heart disease, malnutrition, osteoporosis, or liver disease, may either predate or be the result of chemical dependency. Regardless of its origin, chemical dependency will almost certainly exacerbate an illness. Some studies estimate that between 80 and 86 percent of the older population have at least one chronic health problem.[3]

In attempts to treat themselves or dull their pain, chemically dependent older adults with chronic illnesses are more likely than older adults who are not chemically dependent to take their prescribed medications in combination with alcohol and other medications, perhaps over-the-counter drugs or old, unused prescriptions. It is important for the assessment counselor to ask family members to bring *all* of the older adult's prescribed and over-the-counter drugs to the assessment interview. This will help the intervention team discover what drugs the older adult is using and in what combinations. Family members can also help obtain pharmacy records, which can be helpful in assessing the types and dosages of medication consumed, and may shed light on an older adult's escalation of drug abuse.

---

[3] J. M. McGinnis, "Pioneering Health Promotion: Reaching the Elderly," in *Geriatric Drug Use: Clinical & Social Perspectives*, S. R. Moore and T. W. Teal, eds. (Elmsford, N.Y.: Pergamon Books, 1985), 65; R. B. Weg, *Drug Interaction with the Changing Physiology of the Aged: Practice and Potential* (Los Angeles: University of Southern California Press, 1978), 107.

Assessing Spiritual Problems

"Why deprive my loved one of his final pleasure?" "Why put her through treatment after all the pain she has endured?" are frequently heard statements by those who are close to chemically dependent older adults. The quantity of years, not the quality of life, is misused as a barometer for the appropriateness of intervention and treatment.

When older people lose their vision for life because of chemical dependency, they lose what gives them their sense of direction and purpose. They need help regaining it, regardless of their age. In this sense, chemically dependent older people are no different from other chemically dependent people. They deserve to regain their vision, and this is an important message to convey to family and friends who blame aging as the cause of their loved one's problems and who do not want to deprive them of their drug abuse.

Other issues affecting the spirit of many dependent older adults include grief, shame, and questions such as, "Has God forgiven me?" Dealing with these issues can be especially debilitating for older adults who have done much of their drinking or other drug abuse in isolation. Asking for and accepting help may be especially difficult for someone who has tried to keep his or her drug abuse a secret.

SUGGESTIONS FOR ASSESSMENT TOOLS SPECIFIC TO OLDER ADULTS

It is true that many of the physical and cognitive symptoms of chemical dependency, such as insomnia, malnutrition, physical and cognitive impairment, anxiety, and sadness, may also be seen in older persons who are not chemically dependent. Aging mimics chemical dependency. Chemical dependency mimics aging. Consequently, assessment tools more sensitive to the differences between chemical dependency and aging need to be developed and used for chemically dependent older adults.

There are no assessment tools for the older alcoholic yet. To create them, we need to rely on the team approach to assessment, which includes the cooperation of chemical dependency, medical and nursing, social and psychological, religious, and gerontological disciplines. The gerontologist will be especially helpful on this team. In the past few years, the gerontological field's magazines and journals have addressed the issue of chemical dependency in older adults more frequently than the addiction field has. We have much to learn from each other.

The following list of assessment goals is used for nearly all assessments, but it also includes goals that would be especially helpful in the assessment of chemically dependent older adults.

- To ascertain the intensity and chronicity of the patient's attachment to alcohol and other drugs.
- To determine the nature and pattern of the patient's chemical dependency lifestyle.
- To assess the patient's medical, psychological, physical, developmental, recreational, retirement, and spiritual status, and the patient's ability to care for him- or herself through an activities of daily living assessment.
- To determine which areas of the patient's life have been most severely affected by substance abuse.
- To determine the patient's and his or her family's amenability to treatment and aftercare intervention.
- To prepare a comprehensive plan that will shape treatment activities, guide staff interactions with the patient and his or her family, and shape the patient's peer interactions while in treatment and aftercare.
- To begin discharge planning for transportation needs, meals, and other kinds of care.

Collecting the Information

Collecting information for assessing an older adult usually includes interviewing the patient, his or her family and other friends, and reviewing records of any prior assessments and treatments. Here are more of the usual tools for gathering information.

1. *Medical* – a medical history and physical completed by a physician knowledgeable about geriatric medicine.
2. *Substance abuse history* – collected through a formal assessment questionnaire.
3. *Psychosocial history* – including both a social history and an emotional/behavioral history. In the case of a cognitively impaired older person, this information can be obtained from a friend or relative.
4. *Psychological testing* – focusing primarily on assessing potential neurological damage and deficits in cognitive functioning. Testing instruments may include the Wechsler Memory Scale, Digit Span, Concept Formation Test, Letter Cancellation Test, and Proverbs.
5. *Legal history* – collected for persons who have a history of alcohol-related crimes or are under a guardianship order.
6. *Nutritional assessment* – conducted by a physician or nurse upon admission, and followed by a comprehensive assessment performed by a dietician knowledgeable about geriatric diets.
7. *Leisure assessment* – conducted by an activities consultant to assess how the older patient spends his or her leisure time.
8. *Vocational assessment* – a brief review to collect information that may be used in building rapport with the patient. A more comprehensive vocational assessment should be done for patients who are still employed.
9. *Substance abuse treatment history* – a review of records

related to previous treatment experiences obtained by using standard confidentiality release forms.

10. *Psychiatric evaluation*—to be done when clinically indicated.

11. *Spiritual and religious assessment*—a review of the patient's spiritual and religious beliefs, reasons for living, and feelings about dying. Older adults tend to be more involved in organized religion than younger patients. Guilt, shame, and grief often emerge in this assessment.

12. *Gerontological*—a review of issues proper to aging, including feelings and attitudes about any physical or cognitive impairments, decreased income, mobility, and independence.

13. *Physical therapy assessment*—conducted by a physical therapist to review health concerns related to both aging and alcoholism. Simultaneously treating physical problems and chemical dependency can further a patient's motivation to recover by helping the patient regain mobility and enhance his or her self-esteem.

14. *Staff observation*—performed and documented daily and discussed in interdisciplinary team meetings.

TAKING THE HISTORY OF AN OLDER ADULT

Interviewing older people means handling unique problems, including the patient's, the family's, and the counseling staff's attitudes about older adults and aging. Another big problem can be sensory, physical, and cognitive problems afflicting older adults that hinder good communication. These problems need to be addressed during the interview process if it is to be successful.

Attitudes About Aging

Many attitudes about aging have been formed by myths. In this culture, older persons are often presumed to be unintelligent, mentally incompetent, asexual, unemployable, frail, susceptible to disease, and close to death.[4] These attitudes are formed early in life, and are reinforced by family, culture, religion, and race, although they may be reformed in adulthood.

Try testing your staff's attitudes about aging. Ask them to respond with the first thing that comes to mind when they hear the words "aging," "old," or "elderly." Usually, they will mention the ideals of retirement such as freedom, travel, hobbies, and grandparenting. Then, they may shift to the pains and losses of aging such as lost cognitive ability and health, lost status in the community, trouble with finances, mobility, and transportation, and the death of a spouse, family members, and friends. Many of your peers will say they look forward to the freedoms of growing older and retirement, but they may not be fully aware of the pain and loss they might also feel as they grow older. Chemical dependency professionals need to examine their own attitudes about older adults and aging before they are able to effectively counsel older adults, their families, and friends. Attitudes and feelings about aging are changing and will continue to change as the number of people in our population age sixty-five and older grow.

The Attitude of the Older Person

Emphatic exploration of both aging and chemical dependency stereotypes is time consuming, but it will help everyone involved over the long term of treatment and aftercare. Some people believe that "aging" is a nicer term for the deteriorating physical and mental condition of an older person than "alcoholism" or "chemical dependency." Yet, "aging" is a negative term for many older adults who associate it with weakened

---

[4] M. Logronio, "Overview of Aging Process and Aging Issues," in *Alcohol/Chemical Dependency in the Elderly* (Springfield, Ill.: Illinois Addictions Certification Board, 1987), 36.

sight, hearing, teeth, and physical strength. To some older adults, "aging" may mean that they find it increasingly difficult to perform the activities of daily living such as shopping, cooking, self-care, and hygiene, and the upkeep of their home and property.

Complicating their sensory and physical decline is the cognitive decline many older adults experience, which can cause fears of losing their independence and their way of life, including their home. Older adults are often very resistant to the idea of moving into a child's home, a sheltered care facility, or a nursing home.

This fear of institutionalization and lost freedom may also be associated with an older person's understanding of treatment for alcoholism and drug addiction. Back in the old days, maybe drunken Uncle Harry was placed in the state hospital never to be seen again. For many older adults, "alcoholic" and "drug addict" are terms that conjure up images of weak-willed and degenerate sinners, criminals, or skid row bums. For women, these same terms may conjure images of bad mothers and loose women.

When children have been instrumental in obtaining treatment for their parent, the older adult may often feel betrayed. This can hinder an older person's willingness to cooperate in an interview that he or she suspects is a prelude to institutionalization. Sometimes a family will have obtained a court approved guardianship of the older adult for health care purposes. In these cases, it is difficult to assure the parent, who believes his or her freedom is at stake, that the children are acting out of love and concern. This issue often proves difficult to defuse during treatment, especially if the older person is cognitively impaired.

Similar problems arise if the older person is wealthy or owns a business. In these cases, normal denial can become more deeply entrenched if the older person perceives a threat to his or her finances and business.

An older person may also become concerned about the cost

of treatment. Medicare does not cover the long-term inpatient or residential treatment often needed by older people, who often lack health insurance. It is important for an assessment counselor to be aware of these potential barriers to treatment – to be ready with helpful information about ways to finance treatment, and with an attitude that encourages older adults to seek help.

The Attitude of the Family

Usually, children gain their understanding of chemical dependency and aging from parents. When the children of a chemically dependent older adult confront drug-induced dementia or senility in their parent, childhood understandings of aging and chemical dependency, and memories of how their parents treated the aged and chemically dependent may arise. Not long ago, senile and chemically dependent people were institutionalized in state hospitals or were hidden in their homes. There was little recognition, understanding, or treatment for those whose dementia was due to chemical dependency.

When the children of an older person agree to bring their parent in for a chemical dependency assessment, it is often in response to a stressful event. After the event, it became clear that the only alternatives to treatment were caring for the older person in their own home, assuming the financial burden of hiring someone to provide home care, taking on the physical and emotional burden of providing home care for the parent themselves, or putting their parent in a nursing home. Spouses of chemically dependent people may no longer be able to care for them, and they may also fear losing their own independence if their spouse is institutionalized. Children may have arranged the assessment, yet they may feel anger at having to bear unwanted financial, physical, and emotional burdens related to the care of the dependent parent and spouse.

It is likely that the early-onset alcoholic has alienated his or her family members. Feeling frustrated and defeated in their

29

efforts to help the chemically dependent person, the family may prefer to institutionalize the person, believing that institutionalization will solve their problem. It is also common for some family members of the early-onset alcoholic to be addicted. Ultimately, both the family's desire to distance themselves from the problem and other family members' chemical dependency can hinder the assessment process.

Family members of a late-onset alcoholic often prefer to attribute their loved one's problems to aging rather than to alcohol or other drug abuse. It sounds "nicer" to be providing care for an aging, eccentric, senile parent than it does to be providing care for a chemically dependent parent. Also, children who have not lived with their parents for years may not have observed the drinking or other drug abuse, and they may disbelieve it. Even if they do believe that a parent has become chemically dependent, they may not have much information to offer the assessment counselor.

Family members of both early-onset and late-onset alcoholics may lack an understanding and acceptance of the disease concept of chemical dependency. This is reflected in an often heard question: "Why deprive our loved one of his final pleasure?" When recovering older people are asked what their response to such a question might be, they often respond: "Who said my drinking was pleasurable?" By spending time with uninformed family members, the counselor will gain allies who will grow in their understanding of treatment, become more able to volunteer additional information for the assessment, and become more able to help with discharge and aftercare planning.

The Attitude of the Counselor

Assessment counselors will need to examine their own attitudes toward the stereotypes of aging and older adults. No counselor is so free of biases as to be able to work with all cultural, race, gender, or age groups. A counselor's understanding of his or her own feelings about chemically dependent older adults and their families will help reduce tensions during an assessment.

The results-oriented counselor may feel frustrated with older patients who are slow in their thought processes and who are unable to remain attentive and logical during questions and discussion. Cognitively impaired patients tire easily and will need to be interviewed in short periods of fifteen to twenty minutes. Older adults with physical impairments, such as peripheral neuropathy, may have problems focusing on questions over their discomfort and pain. Older persons with hearing or vision problems, or who have problems with their teeth and gums, may need questions repeated or rephrased. Then, the counselor may be unable to understand a patient's speech because of difficulties caused by their oral problems.

In addition, assessment counselors may feel pressure from other staff or licensing agencies to gather information at the same pace as in the assessment of younger people. This is an unreasonable expectation for counselors to place on themselves, or for other staff or agencies to place on them. Cognitively impaired chemically dependent older people are often unable to meaningfully respond to questions. Family members are not always the best sources for gathering information, so counselors may need to look elsewhere. Medical records are rarely immediately available, and are frequently delayed two to four weeks before release.

Assessment counselors and other staff members may develop a negative attitude toward an older adult patient if they feel they are spending an undue amount of time with him or her. Staff that are unaware of an older adult's unique needs may have difficulty recognizing that the standard assessment schedule of a treatment program does not meet an older person's needs.

Ideally, all counselors would be sensitive to age differences and adjust treatment programs to the slower pace of older patients, but this is not the reality. In many hurry-up treatment modalities, a slow, older adult patient can affect a counselor's schedule. Feelings of impatience with the older person may result. Staff members will need to be certain that a counselor's assessments are age-adjusted, as they are in psychological testing, and that the assessment counselor has taken the necessary time with the patient whose attention span is limited.

Other professionals involved in the assessment process, such as a physical therapist, may also feel rushed given the slower responses of older persons. Older adult patients know when an assessment has been rushed and is not thorough and professional. If they feel that they have been rushed through an assessment, older adults may lose confidence in the treatment process.

COMMUNICATION BARRIERS

Making Sure Older Adult
Patients Can See, Hear, and Speak

If the medical records of an older person do not show a recent examination of his or her mouth, eyes, and ears, you will need to determine how well he or she can speak, see, and hear. The assessment counselor should expect that an older adult's senses have been neglected and dulled due to chemical abuse. Also, an older adult on a fixed income may have decided not to spend money on a new pair of eyeglasses, a new hearing aid, or new, better fitting false teeth, but to make do with an old pair of eyeglasses, hearing aid, or teeth. No assumptions are safe to make. Because an older person has glasses, a hearing aid, or false teeth in his or her possession does not mean that they are useful. A friend or family member may have given him or her the hearing aid or glasses, which might be old and ineffective.

Showing interest in how well they hear and see is sometimes interpreted by older patients as an indication of your interest in them as whole people, not just "that alcohol and drug stuff and prying into my private life." If an older person feels your sincere concern, it will be easier for him or her to develop trust in the assessment process.

For people with impaired sight, soft, indirect lighting will be helpful during the assessment. It may also be helpful to adjust window blinds, shades, or drapes to reduce glare. For people with impaired hearing, place yourself in a position where the patient is able to read your lips. Hearing deficiencies do not automatically come with aging. To test for a hearing deficiency, try asking in a normal voice if the person can understand you. If he or she cannot understand you, ask if the person owns a hearing aid. If the answer is yes, stop the interview so he or she can insert it. To test the hearing aid, have the person run his or her open hand up to the ear with the hearing aid; it should squeal if the volume is appropriate.

When meeting with hearing impaired patients, counselors should avoid rooms with noisy air-conditioning units, frequently ringing telephones, and public address speakers. A counselor should face the patient and speak distinctly so that the patient can read his or her lips. Speaking in a lower tone is more helpful for the hearing impaired than speaking with a louder voice. Do not talk with a pencil in your mouth, or place any item over your lips.

Older people, isolated by their chemical dependency, may not be used to wearing a hearing aid or false teeth. They may complain that the aids are uncomfortable and that they would prefer not to use them. But without teeth, they will have to expend extra energy to pronounce and repeat words, and will have a difficult time conversing with the counselor. This difficulty can try both the counselor's and the patient's patience.

The Physical Condition of the Older Person

It is common for older chemically dependent people to have health problems coexisting with their chemical dependency.

Those who suffer from chronic physical, psychological, emotional, and spiritual pain, expend precious personal energy during the assessment interview. They may have walked or been transported to the interview room, strained their hearing and sight, struggled to speak with ill-fitting teeth, and tried desperately to concentrate and retrieve material from their memory. Simultaneously, they are attempting to subdue their anxiety. An older person in this condition will fatigue easily. Be willing to stop the interview, let the person get some rest, and resume later.

The Cognitively Impaired Older Person

A Case of Severe Cognitive Impairment

> *In 1988, a sixty-four-year-old female patient was transferred by wheelchair from the hospital to the chemical dependency unit of a medical complex; only a set of double doors separated the two units. She had just spent five weeks in the hospital recovering from liver failure. An hour after her arrival on the alcoholism unit, she was asked how she arrived. She claimed she had been brought by ambulance from an old house across town. She then began a monologue about problems she had in her workplace with co-workers, and that at age seventy-four she was old enough to not have to take this work aggravation.*
>
> *Later in the interview, she was asked her age, and she again stated her age as seventy-four. She was asked what year it was and she stated the year to be 1983. Further assessment of her condition was not necessary. Clearly, her immediate need was to gain a basic orientation of who she was, where she was, and what year it was. An assessment of alcoholism could not be made until the patient's cognitive functioning*

34

improved. Also, in order to discover the extent of her
brain damage, a full cognitive assessment was needed.

An older person is more likely than a younger person to suffer from brain damage, liver disease, and malnutrition due to chemical dependency. Consequently, an assessment of cognitive function in the older alcoholic is always recommended.

When interviewing a person suffering from a cognitive impairment, such as an immediate recall disability, the counselor should interpret what the patient says in the simplest manner possible. For example, if a patient seems to answer the counselor's questions without making sense, it could be that the person forgot the question. The counselor should then patiently ask the question again, and ask the patient to repeat it to verify both the patient's hearing and understanding of the question. If the same nonsensical answer is repeated, a counselor can rightly judge that the assessment must be delayed.

Time is necessary to assess any older person, especially when the patient suffers from brain damage. Patients suffering from *alcohol dementia disorder* will show signs of recovery within thirty to sixty days. If mental functioning does not improve after this time, the dementia may be permanent or caused by something else and will need to be treated accordingly.

AN ADDITIONAL ASSESSMENT
SUGGESTED FOR OLDER ADULTS

An Activities of Daily Living Assessment

Having a gerontologist assess an older adult's ability to live independently and handle the activities of daily living will prove beneficial for treatment, discharge, and aftercare planning. This assessment includes questioning the older person and his or her family about the older person's capacity for self-care, which includes the ability to feed oneself and attend to personal hygiene needs. This assessment also includes an evaluation of whether or not sensory aids, such as a hearing aid or glasses, are necessary, and whether the older adult needs help with transportation. Staff observation of the older person while he or she is in treatment can provide valuable clues about the older person's ability to handle the activities of daily living.

A patient's problems with the activities of daily living can ripple out to affect other areas of the patient's life. For example, an older person's sight deficiency, coupled with an observation that he or she walks slowly with the use of a cane, can be indicators that the person will have problems shopping and cooking, which, in turn, could cause a nutritional deficiency. These are important issues to be aware of when beginning discharge planning.

A Physical Therapist's Assessment

A physical therapist's assessment of the older person is also helpful for treatment, discharge, and aftercare planning. In an older person, a physical therapist will typically look for

- range of motion
- agility
- ability to walk as related to peripheral neuropathy
- signs of swelled ankles
- signs of malnourishment
- signs of osteoporosis
- signs of stroke
- signs of muscle deterioration that could affect endurance and the capacity to sit during group therapy and lectures

This assessment can indicate the need for rest periods during the treatment day as well as the need for physical therapy and exercise. Also, the older person's attitudes and feelings about his or her impairments, and their effect on his or her ability to handle the activities of daily living, are important to review, note, and pass along to the treatment team.

36

Conclusion

Assessing older adults for chemical dependency is a new frontier. Symptoms of both aging and chemical dependency are found together in many patients and they can exacerbate each other. Patient, family, and staff attitudes about aging and chemical dependency affect the assessment process. To many people, it is "nicer" to think of an older adult's impairment as an age problem and not a chemical dependency problem.

Chemical dependency is treatable at any age. Assessing chemical dependency in an older adult usually takes more time and patience than assessing chemical dependency in a younger person. But, as with younger people, a quality assessment is the first step in a quality treatment plan. In the end, the extra time it takes to assess older adults is worth it. Treating an older adult's chemical dependency can restore meaning to his or her life and reduce the need for institutionalization.

If we do not know what we are going to be,
we cannot know what we are; let us recognize ourselves
in this old man or in that old woman.
— *Simone de Beauvoir*

CHAPTER THREE

TREATMENT

Margaret Gordon

The treatment process best suited for older adults is difficult to identify partly because chemically dependent older adults defy description as a group. Each older adult is a unique combination of physical and emotional health, family background, vocational and avocational interests, sociological influences, and life experience. The fact that each older person is unique sometimes gets lost in our culture, where older adults are lumped together and viewed as noncontributing members of society. Yet, as with any other generation, older adults do have some common traits. If we are to truly understand chemical dependency in older adults, we must begin to understand how the traits older adults share affect the chemical dependency treatment process.

It is important for treatment professionals to respect the individuality of each older adult patient, but yet have an awareness of what older adults have in common. It would be foolish to suggest that following every approach, suggestion, or modification in this chapter is possible, or even appropriate. Instead, I suggest counselors view the information presented in this chapter as a menu from which they can pick and choose the adaptations that best suit the patient and the structure of their treatment program.

FORMING A TREATMENT PLAN

Some of the greatest differences in treating older adults have to do with physical, social, and family consequences. Older adults' physical health may be severely and permanently affected by alcoholism or other chronic disease, or they may regain their health after an extended detoxification. Social and family networks may be disengaged, enmeshed, or generally dysfunctional, or they may be surprisingly intact. Older adults with chemical dependency problems often remain hidden and isolated from help because of diminished family, work, and social contacts. These realities make each part of the treatment process different for older adults than it is for younger people.

With this in mind, the need for a comprehensive assessment sensitive to older adult issues cannot be emphasized enough. When assessment information is absent, or when the assessment was not sensitive to the needs of older adults, the treatment team will need to complete the assessment process before they can form a long-range treatment plan.

Whether older adults can or should be treated in a particular treatment program depends on the needs of the individual and the structure of the program. Treatment options for older adults are often limited by the scarcity of programs that serve the special needs of older adults and by the high cost of long-term, specialized older adult care. The next best option then, since older adults generally need more time in treatment than thirty-day programs afford, is to find a program that offers extended care, that treats at least a small percentage of older adult patients, and that has demonstrated some awareness of their needs.

Feeling overwhelmed to the point of exhaustion, feeling different, isolated, misunderstood, and stretched beyond capacity is common for anyone entering treatment. But for some older adults, especially those with complicated problems stemming from long-term chemical use and chronic illness, these feelings are even more acute. If they are not resolved with the support of friends, family, and staff, and if they interfere with the therapeutic process, they become serious concerns. Consequently, some older adults may benefit from age-segregated groups.

Bonding with others in the treatment program may be easier for older adults if they are among other older adults. This may also prevent the problem of "mascotting" from occurring. Too often, older adults are enabled by younger members of a treatment program who unwittingly protect and rescue them because of their age and a perception that they are helpless. In such situations, chemical dependency professionals may also find themselves making allowances for their older patients.

Yet, assuming that an older adult will benefit more from being treated with other older adults may also be detrimental. Many older people prefer to be with people of all ages. For active older adults who do not need extended detoxification, and who do not suffer from significant health problems or cognitive impairment, an intergenerational treatment program may be best. Deciding which treatment program is best for an older adult needs to take into account the older adult's needs and the ability of the treatment facility to meet those needs.

ADJUSTING PACE AND INTENSITY

The pace and intensity of a chemical dependency program will need to be adjusted to accommodate the needs of older adults. A treatment day that begins early, moves quickly, and ends late may stretch an older adult's physical and emotional capacity. Many older adults do not have the emotional strength to tolerate long, intense group meetings, and acute or chronic illness may prevent participation until stabilized. Also, the symptoms of extended detoxification – confusion, poor physical condition, anxiety, memory impairment, and sleep disturbances – may prevent an older adult from benefiting from some therapeutic programs.

The answer to many of the challenges of treating older adults is simple: TIME. Many, though not all, older adults need more time than most chemical dependency treatment programs provide. Older adults need time to rebuild their physical strength and emotional reserves; time to build trusting relationships with staff and peers; time free from mood-altering chemicals; time to integrate new information, skills, and behavior and; time for repetition.

Augmenting Care

While the answer, time, is simple, it is not always practical. Chemical dependency professionals, physicians, families, and sometimes patients themselves grow impatient. When push comes to shove, it may be that little can be done to extend the time an older adult has in a structured treatment setting. Yet, it may be impossible to adequately treat a chemically dependent, cognitively or physically impaired older adult in a traditional thirty-day program. Then, creativity is the name of the game. Investigate *any* resources for extending the time an older adult has with therapeutic professionals in a supportive, chemical-free environment. These resources might include:

- extended care
- day treatment
- outpatient programs offered elsewhere within a treatment facility or at another facility
- local resources for seniors, such as adult day care, workshops, and recreation programs that can augment standard care

A willingness to modify treatment schedules, allowing sufficient time for rest during the treatment day, is often a beginning of making a treatment schedule suitable for older adults. Shorter group therapy offered more frequently is better, too, but often unworkable. If groups are of mixed age, working with the older adults first may be helpful if their ability to participate in group diminishes during a long session.

Treatment staff may also have to accommodate an older adult's appointments for medical care. Procedures such as X rays and laboratory tests that are not routinely done for younger adults in treatment may be, for some older adults, a medical necessity that cannot be safely delayed. Scheduling special appointments an older adult may need into an already full day without sacrificing therapeutic groups or activities is a balancing act. An older adult with medical problems may miss out on the important benefits of peer interaction, but an older adult with unresolved medical problems will not be able to, or will not have the motivation to, interact with others.

Cognitively impaired older adults will often need extra attention and guidance to complete routine treatment tasks. If, for example, an older adult is asked to write a history of his or her chemical use and its consequences, the time span of chemical use may cover decades. This sort of assignment can be intimidating for some older adults, and the counselor may need to provide extra time and guidance about how much detail to include.

Varied and flexible educational approaches are usually most effective with cognitively impaired older adults. *Combinations* of reading, audio- and videotapes, journaling, and discussions with staff or peers can make clear their understanding of important concepts such as spirituality or powerlessness. For writing assignments, help from a trusted peer or staff member, or having the option of using a tape recorder, can help older adult patients complete their work.

It is important to ask older patients if they understand their assignments. Cognitive impairment is one concern. Another concern is that older patients have less experience with the language and techniques of therapy, so they may not understand the purpose of an assignment. Gently and privately repeating or reviewing instructions with older adult patients can prevent situations where they feel ashamed or humiliated because they have misunderstood directions.

Treatment counselors will need to be very clear about the basic concepts and expectations of the treatment process. An older adult's progress in understanding treatment concepts may be steady but slow. Changing patterns of behavior developed over decades take a lot of time and a lot of effort. Reminding older adults of this fact affirms and validates their progress. A supportive environment that allows older adults to progress at their own rate is important. Patience – on everyone's part – is a virtue.

ADDRESSING SENSORY IMPAIRMENT

Because some vision and hearing impairment are common in older adults, communicating may require special effort from the counselors and older adults. Staff members should not assume that an older adult patient can hear, see, read, or write, or that they will readily admit that they have any problems doing so. Staff members need to ascertain – through direct questioning and observation – if their patients are able to hear and see adequately, and to arrange for a hearing or vision screening if hearing or vision problems exist.

Adjusting Treatment For
Patients with Impaired Hearing

Hearing deficits cause problems with group dynamics and may limit the ability of the older adult patient to participate. For example, when some people deal with intense emotional issues, they often look down, and their voices become very quiet; their words slur, tears fall. This kind of circumstance is difficult for the hearing impaired person, but is common in group sessions. Communicating with hearing impaired people is best done face to face so they can lip read, and with a loud, strong, deep voice, and clearly pronounced words.

During group sessions, older adults may not request that others speak up for a number of reasons. They may feel ashamed of their disability. They may not wish to interrupt and appear uncaring or rude to the person who is speaking. On the other hand, lack of motivation, denial, and *selective deafness* may be the problem. Choosing not to hear, or refusing to admit a hearing problem, are effective ways to avoid dealing with intense feelings or difficult information.

Unfortunately, there is no magic solution for differentiating when a patient chooses not to hear and when he or she is physically unable to hear. Carefully observe the person's response to attempts to improve the situation. Try to decrease background noise in meeting areas, or amplify speakers in group sessions with a microphone. Remember, a deeper voice is better heard than a higher voice. Counselors with higher voices can lower them and project better to compensate. Also, speak slowly and distinctly without exaggerating mouth movements, and speak face to face. In some patients, the problem may be resolved simply by ensuring that hearing aids work and are worn. Validate their understanding of instructions by having them repeat or review them.

Adjusting Treatment For Patients with Impaired Sight

For older adults with impaired vision, reading and writing assignments may be difficult, if not impossible. Vision problems may be exaggerated due to denial and avoidance, making it difficult to determine the true extent of the disability. There is no easy way to assess whether vision is so deteriorated that an older adult is incapable of reading an assignment, and the possibility of hidden illiteracy should be considered.

To ensure that older adults with impaired vision participate in and benefit from treatment, it is important to provide assignments, adaptive equipment, and rehabilitation that is sensitive to their needs. Simple solutions include

- making large-print materials available.
- using audiotapes.
- having the option of using a tape recorder in place of a pencil and paper.
- posting large-print signs, maps, or symbols that help the visually impaired person find his or her way around the treatment center.
- leaving personal possessions in specific places so they can be easily found.
- using the buddy system to complete assignments.

Treatment center staff may wish to use community resources for the hearing and visually impaired. State services and charitable agencies can provide adaptive equipment for the hearing and visually impaired. Instruction on how to use adaptive equipment is often available through these same resources, as well as training for treatment center staff.

Attention to safety details, such as keeping hallways clear of obstruction, installing handrails, and providing adequate lighting, even at night, may prevent falls or other injuries. Remembering that hearing or visually impaired patients may not hear fire alarms or see exit signs in an emergency can avoid potential tragedy.

Adjusting Treatment for Patients with Aphasia

Aphasia is a special communication problem that affects the understanding of speech or the formulation of speech. People who suffer from *expressive aphasia* may be unable to find the appropriate words to express themselves, substituting instead words that make no sense. People with *receptive aphasia* do not understand words or phrases–their brain simply does not receive the message correctly. Aphasia results in confusion, frustration, ᵃnd reluctance to attempt self-expression.

Mabel's Story

> *Mabel was admitted to treatment about six months after her head injury resulted in aphasia. Though Mabel could understand everything said to her, most of her communication took the form of gestures and pointing. During early group meetings, the first phrase out of her mouth was "I can't!" Initially, group members supplied words for her and rescued her by filling the silences. Gradually, the group of older adults became more comfortable with silence as they patiently waited for Mabel to express herself. Though Mabel was able to speak only short phrases, her few words expressed her emotions quite eloquently.*

Aphasic older adults may appear much more disabled and cognitively impaired than they really are. Their memory and reasoning ability are often completely intact. A great deal of patience is required of staff, and other patients, because self-expression is truly difficult for aphasic patients. Each sentence may take minutes to speak. During painful, emotional times, or when under a lot of stress, their speech can become unintelligible. Supplying words for aphasic patients is not always helpful, since the rehabilitation process requires them to learn to speak again. When severe, aphasia may prevent a patient from any participation in treatment because of the necessity of verbalization. Chemically dependent older adults with less severe aphasia can be treated in an atmosphere of acceptance, by keeping verbal expression simple, and by using creative, alternative assignments. A feelings chart, for example, might be used to help name and identify feelings.

Other speech impediments, whether due to a chronic condition or recent injury, may also be addressed by an atmosphere of acceptance, by allowing adequate time for expression and repetition, and by allowing time for patients to deal with feelings of shame, anger, or self-pity that may accompany efforts to communicate.

Chemical dependency professionals need to educate themselves about disabilities, their causes, and their physical and emotional effects. More specifically, they need to educate themselves about how to effectively counsel chemically dependent older adults who suffer from a range of mental and physical impairments.

ADDRESSING CHRONIC DISEASE
AND OTHER HEALTH PROBLEMS

Chronic illness and other health problems often have an effect on the treatment and recovery processes of older adults. Some of the more common disorders likely to afflict chemically dependent older adults include:

- heart disease
- diabetes
- hypertension
- arthritis
- chronic lung diseases
- liver impairment
- gastrointestinal disorders

Much as chemical dependency does, these diseases can affect every sphere of an older adult's life – self-image, relationships, social, recreational, and financial.

John's Story

> *John's alcoholism started well before his stroke. In fact, his first treatment experience, six years prior, resulted in eighteen months of sobriety. During stroke rehabilitation efforts, he remained abstinent, but his alcoholism was not addressed. The stroke left him with a residual left-sided weakness. He was able to walk with a cane, but relied on a wheelchair for long distances.*
>
> *His alcohol use after rehabilitation caused such severe deterioration of his condition that he was no longer able to care for himself. He spent his days angry and depressed, seeking relief from the physical and emotional pain, the boredom and frustration, in alcohol.*
>
> *It became apparent that dealing effectively with John's chemical dependency required some resolution of the self-image issues related to his stroke. His treatment plan was updated to include grief work with the chaplain about his physical losses. Daily affirmations and self-esteem building assignments were added to improve John's self-worth and self-image. A nurse from a local home health care agency dedicates a half hour each day to helping John relearn adaptive techniques he previously used. The aftercare plan was also altered to include attendance at a stroke survivor's support group.*

Some of the ideas used in recovery from chemical dependency are also used in chronic disease management:

- Acknowledging loss of control
- Working through denial
- Acceptance of powerlessness and unmanageability
- Dealing with depression, anger, guilt, and shame
- Seeking spiritual guidance
- Working a daily program of health and spiritual wellness

Whether or not rehabilitation for a chronic disease is needed during treatment or as a part of aftercare is a decision best made by a physician who understands the role chemical dependency plays in a patient's illness. Sometimes, the focus on recovery from chemical dependency gets fragmented by rehabilitative care. Or, the treatment center may be unable or unwilling to provide this care due to the lack of resources or qualified staff. At other times, rehabilitative care may be absolutely necessary if recovery from chemical dependency is to begin. Assessing both the patient and the treatment facility's ability to meet a person's needs is the key to resolving this dilemma successfully.

The most important factor in providing physical care for older adults is a *nonjudgmental, nurturing attitude* that encourages patients to function their best. There is a very fine line between care*giving* and care*taking* older adults with the dual problems of chemical dependency and chronic disease.

COMPLICATING FACTORS

The issues of extended detoxification, depression, and cognitive impairment can greatly complicate the process of chemical dependency treatment. There are steps the therapeutic professional can take to assure that his or her patients are receiving the care they need.

Jane's Story

> *Even after an initial assessment and days of detoxification, Jane still had a poor appetite, short attention span, disturbed sleep patterns, and was confused. These symptoms became particularly severe at night. She was often sad, she cried almost daily, and she felt hopeless. She had trouble recalling simple details and often answered questions with an apathetic "I don't*

know." It was unclear whether Jane really didn't know or if she didn't care to answer. She denied that she had memory problems, denied that she felt depressed, and denied her alcoholism.

Jane is a type of patient commonly encountered by counselors of chemically dependent older adults. In the first two or three weeks of abstinence, symptoms like Jane's may be a sign of extended detoxification, depression, or cognitive impairment. Determining which problem is the primary cause of the symptoms is difficult because extended detoxification, depression, and cognitive impairment are seldom seen in isolation. The range of severity of cognitive impairment is nearly infinite. In addition, confusion that appears to be irreversible dementia may, in fact, be due to extended detoxification. Also, depression is often masked by confusion and behavior usually indicative of cognitive impairment called *pseudodementia.*

The Myth of Natural Cognitive Decline

Older adults attempt to compensate for cognitive deficits— they may present themselves as confident and capable. If the impairment is mild, they may be able to successfully hide it; but if the impairment is moderate to severe, the facade falls apart quickly. Unfortunately, many family members, friends, and therapists fail to see through an older adult's attempt to cover for his or her cognitive impairment, so they blame the older adult's behaviors and attitudes on a lack of motivation or denial when cognitive impairment is the real problem. With all this confusion, what can a counselor do? The most important thing to remember for everyone working with older adults is that *confusion, disorientation, and memory loss are not normal parts of aging.*

When confusion, disorientation, and memory loss appear, it is the result of a disease process of some kind. People should not expect to grow feeble-minded and forgetful as they age.

Whether a cognitive decline is due to chronic disease, acute infection, detoxification, depression, or any other cause, it needs to be completely and thoroughly investigated. Confusion and cognitive impairment may, indeed, be the first signs of progressive dementia, but they should never be considered normal, age-related changes.

Realistic Expectations

When cognitive impairment, depression, and extended detoxification complicate the course of chemical dependency treatment, it is very difficult for the clinician to ensure that appropriate care is delivered. Sorting through these issues depends on the ability of the multidisciplinary team to follow through with the ongoing responsibility of monitoring and observing older adult patients. The psychological evaluation and psychiatric examination are particularly important for determining the level of depression and cognitive impairment and for recommending what treatments are necessary and which therapeutic approaches might be most effective. With this knowledge, the counselor will be better able to set realistic expectations of progress.

Determining the risk for suicide must be a part of the psychological evaluation, since older adults – especially white males – have a very high suicide rate. Remember, too, that older adults are at high risk for other self-destructive behaviors, including refusing to take their medication, refusing to eat and care for themselves, and engaging in reckless and unsafe behavior. When suicide is identified as a high risk in an older adult, they, like any other person, will need a comprehensive plan of care to provide for safety and reduce the risk of suicide.

The Importance of Timing

Timing is a crucial factor in the treatment process. The multidisciplinary team needs to be aware that older adults may suffer from symptoms of extended detoxification during the entire course of treatment. Until these symptoms are alleviated, it may be unclear whether treatment of depression with antidepressant medication is needed. If medication is needed, it may take from two to three weeks for the level of depression to improve. Unfortunately, most chemical dependency treatment programs simply cannot provide the length of stay necessary to ensure the most appropriate care. Because treatment time is so short, aftercare planning is also affected. Neither treatment for chemical dependency nor treatment for depression will be effective without ongoing psychiatric monitoring of depression and ongoing support for sobriety.

Working with older clients who have symptoms of depression or cognitive impairment will require a lot of patience from the multidisciplinary team. Close supervision is critical in providing for the patient's physical health and safety. Repetition of basic concepts can be tedious, but is often required. Scaling down assignments and goals may be necessary. Also, abstract reasoning and the ability to form concepts and insights may be severely limited in older adults with cognitive impairment who also suffer from depression. Using treatment phrases such as " internalizing powerlessness and unmanageability" may not work for many older adults. Instead, using the most basic tenets of the Twelve Step program, such as the AA slogans Keep it Simple, First Things First, Let Go and Let God, and the *Serenity Prayer* can help impaired older adults achieve sobriety, peace, and serenity.

GENERATIONAL BARRIERS

Older adults' perception that they are being treated in a dignified and respectful manner is an important ingredient in their understanding and acceptance of the treatment process. Language they perceive as harsh, a style of dress they view as excessively casual or seductive, and dormitory-style living may be readily accepted by younger adults, but it may offend older adults. Older adults may prefer to be called Mr. or Mrs. rather than by their first name or a nickname. Older adults entering a therapeutic setting for the first time may not understand the language of therapy. Phrases such as "stay with the feeling," "taking time in group," "working a program," "Higher Power," and "chemical of choice" may require explanation. Even the noise and activity level of a residential or inpatient unit may be distracting and stressful.

Worst of all, an older adult is unlikely to be assertive about what is distracting or stressful to them. Some older adults behave in people-pleasing, overly compliant ways; they wish to do things the "proper" way and prefer to avoid being the center of attention. They don't want to feel burdensome or patronized.

Offering older adults assistance and support to deal with new and changing situations is better than waiting for them to seek assistance or clarification on their own. Using the buddy system for the first few days may also help older adults feel more comfortable with finding directions, following the daily schedule, clarifying expectations, and building relationships. Some older adults may feel as if they have little in common with chemically dependent younger people. Assigning a younger adult to be a buddy to an older adult may help the older adult feel more a part of treatment and may be valuable for the younger adult as well.

Tuning in to the physical boundaries of an older adult is another important part of dignified and respectful treatment. Some older adults may have a long history of not expressing emotions, of being stoic, and many may be quite rigid about being touched by and touching staff or peers. Staff may not be aware of any unresolved abuse issues, since these are often carefully guarded secrets. Some older adults may be quite "touch starved," because they have not had physical contact for a long time and do not know how to initiate or receive it.

Moving slowly and asking permission are simple solutions, and their importance cannot be underestimated.

THE THERAPEUTIC PROCESS

Building the Counselor/Patient Relationship

Building a good counselor/patient relationship with older adults is not all that different from building a good therapeutic relationship with other patients. It is very important for older adults to sense that their counselor is sincerely interested in them and is patient and willing to devote enough time and energy to the relationship.

Time helps build quality and effective therapeutic relationships. It may take longer for older adults to develop trust enough to disclose sensitive information. Older adults usually begin slowly, telling only a little about their feelings to a few. This needs to be respected. Patients who feel rushed or hurried may feel as if they are taking others' time and are burdensome, which can trigger feelings of shame and low self-esteem. Remember that a patient's perception of being rushed is real to him or her, even if it does not seem that way to the counselor.

Setting a time limit on individual therapy may help an older adult focus more clearly and more wisely use individual therapy. Rambling repetitions of previously disclosed information need not be a problem if the counselor guides the person into more relevant discussion. Yet, sometimes relaying intricate detail is very important to the older adult.

Building Skills for Self-Disclosure and Risk Taking

Sharing feelings and sensitive information may be unfamiliar to older adults participating in a therapy group for the first time. To help them feel at ease, start by asking them to disclose safe information and work toward helping them disclose more sensitive, risky information. Early assignments should not be intimidating. Possibly a "get to know me" assignment, including a series of questions about career, upbringing, education, or other information the older adult may choose to reveal would be a good beginning.

Clear expectations of participation, including risk taking, confrontation, and support, should be set early in treatment. Also, take the time to thoroughly explain confidentiality and anonymity, and make sure older adults understand these and other treatment concepts by asking them what their understanding is. Taking time to do this may provide comfort to ill-at-ease older adults.

Having a good reputation and keeping personal problems private are strongly held values of many older adults. They may not share problems and feelings even with family or intimate friends. Reviewing with them confidentiality policies may help them feel safe, more at ease. Ultimately, acknowledging that progress toward self-disclosure and risk taking is slower for many older adults will help the counselor to more appropriately assess their progress and accommodate their pace.

Development of Group Dynamics

In groups where there are only one or two older adults, the group facilitator will need to watch how well the older adults participate. They may be quite passive, allowing themselves to be excluded from intense interaction and discussion. They may seem to sit on the periphery, watching but not participating. Group assignments designed to promote trust may be needed to bring older adults more actively into group interaction. Sensitivity to the special needs of older adults needs to be shown by staff *and* peers.

On the other hand, the role of the group facilitator when the

56

majority of group members are older is more direct and requires a lot of energy. They may be frustratingly silent and noninteractive at times. But with positive role modeling, clear expectations of participation, and some time to get comfortable with the group process, an older adult may become a valuable member to a dynamic group.

Overall, stressing that each group member needs to participate and encouraging patience and sensitivity to the needs of others will help build a dynamic, therapeutic group.

Peer Feedback and Support

Some older adults behave in nonassertive, overly compliant, enabling ways. In an effort to avoid confrontation, they choose to negate their own needs and tolerate the negative attitudes and behaviors of those around them. After years of behaving this way, they may not recognize their own needs, and, as a result, their resentments, anger, and frustrations may have to build to an intense level before they risk sharing these feelings. Older adults may also fear hurting someone else's feelings, so they often have difficulty giving feedback they perceive as negative.

Receiving feedback may be equally difficult. Depending on the older adult's sensitivity, *any* feedback may be perceived as hurtful and negative, depending on who offers it and the tone of voice. Feedback perceived as negative may be met with rigid defensiveness, passive resistance, and defiance. Patients with cognitive impairment may not understand the feedback, and patients with impaired hearing may not hear it. Neither is likely to ask for clarification; they both want to avoid further confrontation.

Even giving positive feedback to peers may be difficult for older adults. They often offer statements like, "You're such a nice person" in place of more meaningful feedback about a peer's specific personal attributes or accomplishments. Older adults may also have problems receiving positive peer feedback. If their self-worth is low, they may not believe affirming, supportive statements. Or, they may choose to disregard them. Gracefully receiving and believing compliments, positive feedback, and support without self-deprecating comments is a learned behavior. As self-esteem builds, patients are more able to learn this behavior.

Helping to develop an older adult's ability to give and receive feedback can be a slow process. Older adults need to hear over and over again that feedback they perceive as negative is not meant to hurt others, but is meant to help others change negative, destructive behaviors. Older adults learn, like everyone else, through experience and role modeling that giving feedback helps much more than remaining silent.

Confrontation

Confrontation in a gentle, nurturing way is important for anyone who has a great deal of shame or anger. Many chemically dependent older adults have a lot of shame and anger. Older adults often fear confrontation, so it is important that a counselor's tone of voice, language, posture and stance, and gestures be nonthreatening. For clarification, some older adults may need to hear the difference between open, honest observations and angry attacks. They may recall hearing about or may have even experienced the "hot seat."

When older adults are confronted in front of others, they may feel humiliated and shamed and are likely to respond by withdrawing and by being defensive. A more gentle and effective approach for older adults is to first raise issues in an individual session, taking an educational approach and providing guidance by pointing out self-defeating behaviors and attitudes, and then suggesting positive alternative behaviors. A short walk outside may be one way of reducing tension and formality. Maintaining eye contact, speaking softly, and using supportive touch, such as a hand on the shoulder or forearm, may put a patient at ease and reduce defensiveness.

Counselors should not assume that their message is accurately received, no matter how simply stated. It is important for the counselor to check the patient's understanding by asking him or her to explain the message. Restatement of some messages is often needed to ensure accurate perception and to make clear the changes in behavior that are needed.

SHAME

Feelings of shame affect many chemically dependent older adults in a very fundamental way. Older adults who are products of the Temperance movement and Prohibition often believe alcoholism is an issue of morality rather than a disease. With this in mind, it is no surprise that defense mechanisms such as denial and delusion are so strong in chemically dependent older adults. Because of their upbringing, they usually see only two choices for dealing with the facts and consequences of their chemical abuse. One choice is to rationalize, minimize, and deny the effects of the abuse. The other is to admit to being morally degenerate, shameful, and worthless.

Helping to reduce an older adult's high level of shame will probably be done gradually, and small advances can mean significant progress. Even introducing oneself as an alcoholic in a therapy group or Alcoholics Anonymous meeting may be intensely shameful. Though some may see this as evidence of denial, it may also be an indication of intense shame.

Presentation of the disease concept and the basic tenets of the Twelve Step philosophy should be done slowly, carefully, and repeatedly. It is worth the time it takes to make sure older adults understand the ideas being communicated to them.

Older adults often have other issues in their lives that produce feelings of shame. Chronic disease and disability, sensory impairments, cognitive dysfunction, and a lack of productive employment may lead to feelings of worthlessness in our society that reveres beauty, youth, fitness, and career. It is critically important for chemically dependent older adults to have help building self-esteem and dealing with multiple shame issues. Exposing them to role models of successfully recovering older adults – whether a staff member or a person in literature or a video – can be an effective way of showing that change is possible.

SELF-ESTEEM

Building self-esteem is an important part of any therapeutic process, but it can be especially important for older adults. Showing them how to build on their strengths, and teaching them positive coping skills for their limitations, will enhance the quality of their recovery. Using daily affirmations and positive support from peers is a good way to help older adults gain self-worth and self-esteem. Also, recognition and celebration of small successes builds confidence and the willingness to tackle more difficult tasks.

Chemically dependent older adults, especially those whose dependency is more chronic in nature, may have problems viewing their past as meaningful and worthwhile. Since they may have been using chemicals for forty or fifty years, they probably have more negative experiences than positive achievements.

One valuable way to build self-esteem in these older adults is through the use of *therapeutic reminiscence.* Helping older adults review their life's events encourages them to reestablish their identity and to reintegrate past events into their personality and self-image. Therapeutic reminiscence can help them gain perspective on their disease by helping them recall positive events, old disappointments, and the feelings that accompany those memories. With a counselor's help, older adults can look at the positive side of their past and choose to feel good about their contributions, and about the opportunity to build on those in recovery.

Reminiscence helps older adults reconcile hopes and dreams with realities, but it is not the best time to confront denial and delusion. Story telling can be very therapeutic, but it may also be used to avoid and deny issues that need resolution. It is important not to dwell solely on the destructive aspects of the dependency. Care should be taken to validate an older adult's contributions and affirm his or her self-worth.

EXPRESSING FEELINGS

Healthy expression of feelings is one of the fundamentals on which chemical dependency treatment is based. Expressing feelings is particularly important for older adults who were often taught to hide their feelings, especially those viewed as negative. Anger, fear, shame, sadness, grief, inadequacy, regret, and pride are feelings that may have been closeted away, left unexpressed. Many older adults were taught that it was desirable to control their emotions, to be rigid and stoic, and to always make an effort to maintain emotional composure. Repeated denial of emotional expression rapidly becomes an inability to identify feelings. Many older adults still believe that feelings and problems should be kept private, away from everyone, even other family members. Obviously, these beliefs severely limit the potential for healthy expression and sharing.

Older adults feel the same reluctance and fear about confronting emotional pain as younger adults. Like them, they need emotional support. But unlike them, older adults are less likely to seek comfort in staff or their peers in treatment. Some younger or older peers in treatment, peers whose intentions are kindhearted but misguided, may protect and enable older adults to avoid intense feelings. One gentle way to get older adults to deal with intense feelings is to, at first, give them assignments where they confront only "safe" emotions. Then, as their successes accumulate, they can slowly begin working on assignments in which they confront more difficult and intense feelings.

GRIEF

Grief and loss may pervade the life of an older adult. Every sphere of their life–physical, emotional, social, and economic–may be affected by the changes that accompany aging. Most often these changes are associated with loss rather than attainment. When an older adult has experienced loss in several areas, grief is compounded.

One result of the assessment process is to determine what losses the patient has suffered and where he or she is in the grieving process. Based on this information, the counselor can make a reasonable estimate of the progress that can be made on unresolved grief issues. Sometimes, grief issues block progress in chemical dependency treatment and adjunctive psychotherapy is required. Ongoing grief work may also become an aftercare issue.

Grieving takes time, and the impact of supportive therapy and education will not produce immediate results unless sufficient time is allowed to work through the grief. Small steps toward grief resolution should be celebrated and supported in order to encourage further progress in the grieving process.

A grief group can be a helpful therapeutic tool. In these groups, older adults can find the support of peers who have experienced similar losses and share their feelings with them. Simple information about the stages of grieving may be very helpful to an older adult, especially for those trying to understand their feelings of anger. During the course of treatment, the older adult may, for the first time, be forced to deal with feelings about major losses and the more subtle grief issues of aging. They may express anger and rage, as well as intense sadness and despair. For older adults, working with a clergy-person may provide comfort and reassurance.

No Special Allowances

The counselor needs to be aware of his or her attitude about grief and older people. It is normal to feel sad and sympathetic as older adults describe their sorrow and anguish. Grieving older adults often seem very, very fragile. Consequently, counselors sometimes begin to make allowances for older adults in this tragic emotional state. (Grief, however, is seldom used as a manipulative tool; few grieving older people will ask for the diminished expectations they are sometimes granted.) It is here that counselors should be very careful. Empathy is extremely important in working with grieving older adults, but attitudes that result in special allowances for the grieving older adult are only a whisper away from the belief, *If I lost everything they did, I'd drink too.*

SPIRITUALITY

Encouraging spirituality in older adults is different than it is with other age groups. Younger people are more likely to enter treatment internally empty, devoid of spirituality, and disillusioned with organized religion. Older adults, because of their addiction, also enter treatment internally empty and devoid of spirituality, but with a wide variety of religious experience and values. Older adults who retain no religious affiliation are likely to have difficulty with the concept of a Higher Power, believing that it is only a disguise for religion. Conversely, those who were born and raised within an organized religion are likely to have difficulty being open to concepts of spirituality and Higher Power other than how God is seen by their particular denomination. Mary had this problem.

Mary's Story

Mary, who was in a great deal of denial about her alcoholism, believed that "good Catholics" are not alcoholics. Throughout her pathological drinking, she practiced traditional sacred rituals, though she seemed to gain little spiritual comfort from them. In treatment, she became very uncomfortable with a peer's discussion of her relationship with a feminine deity, and was openly suspicious and distrustful of another peer who proclaimed himself a devout atheist. She had problems discerning the difference between spirituality and religion, and often felt as though her religious beliefs were being attacked or criticized. Somehow, misinterpreting information about spirituality, Mary had the notion that she must completely abandon her religious beliefs to stay sober.

Both the counselor and chaplain worked with Mary. Their goal was to increase her awareness of the differences between spirituality and religion, and to help Mary be more tolerant of and open to others. They were careful to respect her religious beliefs and tried to help her see other possibilities. Fortunately, a recovering priest was able to help Mary see how her religion fit with the spiritual part of the Twelve Step program. Eventually, her religion became an integral part of her spirituality.

Understanding what spirituality is, and how to find it, is an integral part of the recovery process. Promoting spiritual growth, while respecting many older adults' deeply ingrained religious beliefs, is a great challenge because they might not see the distinction between spirituality and religion. So they will not dismiss them out of hand, older adults will need encouragement to keep an open mind while exploring new options and discussing alternative belief systems.

Care should be taken to provide time and areas for quiet meditation and reflection. Some older adults may choose to use religious rituals and symbols that are uncomfortable for others. To avoid the discomfort, using a meditation book or guide may be more helpful than a daily prayer book. Any of the wide variety of available daily meditation guides will suffice. Some meditation books are available in large print and some also have audiotape versions. Many older adults will also wish to attend worship services at a local church of their choice.

SOCIALIZATION AND RECREATION

Alcoholism tends to isolate its victims from their social support networks. And with older adults, this network may already be tenuous from changes associated with aging. Too often, older adults withdraw from social contact because of embarrassment or frustration about cognitive impairment or physical problems, such as hearing or vision impairment, difficulty with walking and climbing stairs, or stress incontinence. Also, the pressures of living on a fixed income may limit many older adults' ability to spend money on hobbies, crafts, or other activities, such as bowling, golf, or travel that bring them together with other people. All of these problems can narrow the circle of significant, close relationships an older adult has. The effects of a spouse's death, friends dying or becoming ill, and chronic disease or physical disability tend to isolate some older adults precisely when they need their social networks the most.

Leisure skills education can help older adults explore new interests, or reignite enthusiasm for former favorites. It is important to enlist their help and enthusiasm when putting together a plan. To combat isolation, encourage participation in social events that will get them together with other people. Conducting a search for handicap-accessible facilities within the community may give the chemically dependent older adult more resources for aftercare planning. Taking a trial run at sober socialization often helps older adults gain confidence for reentering an old social network or creating a new one.

A detailed socialization and recreation plan is an important recovery tool for older adults. It helps fill hours of the day that were formerly spent drinking or using other drugs. When writing a socialization and recreation plan for an older adult patient, the counselor needs to remember to consider physical limitations, income, and personal interests. Enlisting the support of a sponsor or concerned family members in carrying out the plan is helpful, and sometimes necessary. Counselors should remember too that a socialization and recreation plan must also be fun.

✳ ✳ ✳ ✳ ✳

Flexibility and patience are the two most important qualities a counselor and the multidisciplinary team needs to provide effective chemical dependency treatment to older adults. A staff member's willingness to modify the structure of his or her program and use techniques adapted to meet older adults' needs is critical. Patiently listening to older adults is therapeutic for them, and often provides benefits for the staff member as well. It is essential to meet the older adult where they are and to encourage them to grow to their fullest potential, whatever that potential is. An atmosphere of nonjudgmental nurturing that supports limitations and builds on strengths can be developed.

The proportion of this country's population over age sixty is growing rapidly, and, in coming years, the characteristics of this population will change greatly due to societal changes over the past fifty years. Professionals need to educate themselves to prepare for the growth in this population group, but they also need to remain open to new approaches as the characteristics and commonalties of older adults change, and as new information and research becomes available.

Age is not all decay;
it is the ripening, the swelling, of the fresh life within,
that withers and bursts the husk.
— George Macdonald

CHAPTER FOUR

CONTINUING CARE

Mary Marrs Holmes, L.S.W

Joyce's Story

Although Joyce was strictly a social drinker through
middle age, in her late sixties, after her husband's
death, she began to occasionally rely on alcohol to relieve depression and insomnia. Her drinking pattern
shifted further when she discovered that alcohol also
eased the pain of her arthritis. On particularly painful
days, she would take a drink to relieve her morning
stiffness. Within a few months, the insomnia, arthritis,
and the new pain of hangovers were ample reason for
Joyce to drink every day.

One day, Joyce fell at home and was taken to the
emergency room. While under observation at the
hospital, she began to exhibit classic signs of alcohol
withdrawal. Her family was shocked. Even her doctor
was surprised. Joyce's detoxification was complicated
by her poor nutrition and generally weak condition.
Even walking was difficult for her. She was confused,
incontinent, and she hallucinated. Her mood fluctu-
ated from depression and anger to paranoia.

*As the detoxification process progressed, her inconti-
nence disappeared, her walking improved, and most of
Joyce's psychiatric symptoms abated, although she
continued to be depressed. The detox staff talked to her
about the need for treatment. She didn't believe she had
a problem with alcohol. After all, she didn't drink that
much and surely didn't act like a drunk. Finally, she
agreed to give treatment a try; it was important to her
daughters, and besides, she needed care and time to
recuperate from her fall.*

*Treatment was a whirlwind of activity: groups, as-
signments, and so many new people. While she enjoyed all the company, Joyce was appalled by the vul-
gar language and stories some of the younger patients
told about their chemical abuse. The treatment center
staff encouraged her to share her own story, but when
she tried, the words just wouldn't come. As she had
aged, she felt her life had become less interesting—both
to her and to others. Besides, she was embarrassed to
show her dirty laundry in public.*

*Joyce had always believed that if you're going to do
something, you should do it well. So, in treatment, she
tried her best. It was hard for her to stay with the pace
and understand all the treatment jargon, but she did
manage to complete the first three steps of AA. She became friends with some of the other patients. A few
even called her Grandma.*

*Almost before she knew it, Joyce was discharged. The
treatment center staff stressed the importance of aftercare groups and AA, and Joyce nodded in agreement.
An AA group met just a few miles from her home, and
she planned to attend an aftercare group as well.*

*Joyce returned home feeling good. She was still con-
fused about the language of treatment and what*

recovery was all about, but she knew she wanted sobriety and needed people around her.

Joyce's daughter agreed to drive her to doctor's appointments and aftercare meetings. Her other daughter took her to her first AA meeting and waited outside. She felt frightened to be among a group of strangers, but a few people were friendly and she didn't feel pressure to speak up. After a couple of weeks, Joyce started to feel guilty about having to depend on her daughters so much. In treatment, Joyce looked forward to being home, but now she found it lonely and depressing. Reminders of her late husband and the busy days when they were raising the girls filled the home. She wanted to talk with others, but she had lost touch with most of her friends. Her daughters were busy, and she was reluctant to bother them. She didn't call her good friend Millie because she didn't want her to know she'd been in treatment.

Mealtimes were the worst. Joyce hated eating alone. It was too much work to make a complete meal, so she got in the habit of having toast and jelly. Sometimes she just heated soup and ate it from the pot.

One of the younger people Joyce met in treatment called to see how she was, and that felt good, although after a bit there wasn't much to talk about. Her young friend was busy with her job, new friends from AA, and she and Joyce didn't have much in common.

The next week, Joyce's daughter had a sick child and couldn't drive her to AA. She thought of calling a cab, but that was too expensive. Joyce didn't know anyone in AA well enough to ask them for a ride. She thought they wouldn't understand anyway.

The support and energy she felt while in treatment seemed far away. Most days, Joyce didn't see anyone, and there seemed little point in getting dressed or tidying up the house. Joyce knew her daughters were con-

cerned, but she felt if they really loved her, they would take better care of her. Joyce quit attending aftercare groups. She didn't get much out of the sessions, and didn't like to be out at night. The aftercare counselor was worried, but Joyce just didn't know how to explain to her what was wrong.

Joyce's wedding anniversary was coming up; she couldn't sleep, thinking about her husband and everything that had happened since he died. Finally, tired, depressed, and desperately needing to sleep, Joyce thought, Just one drink, I'll only have one. She called the local liquor store, ordered her favorite, and had it delivered.

The driver was very nice, saying, "Where have you been, Joyce? We've missed you and were afraid you might be sick. I'm glad you're okay."

COMING TOGETHER TO MEET OLDER ADULTS' NEEDS

Joyce's sobriety was short-lived because her treatment and aftercare plan did not meet her needs as an older adult. She had no real peers in treatment; few people could relate to her experiences. Furthermore, society's stereotypes and biases about older adults were active in the treatment center; Joyce was not encouraged—nor expected—to share her story and process her feelings to the same extent that other, younger group members were. Because the treatment staff had little knowledge about older adults' treatment issues, they did not recognize the depth of Joyce's isolation and the shame she felt about her alcoholism. Nor did they understand how difficult it was for her to ask for help.

Issues that seem relatively minor for many people may be nearly insurmountable for older adults. Many older adults wonder and worry about things that would not worry a younger adult.

- "How will I get to AA meetings twice a week?"
- "I can't tell strangers about my problems. I wasn't raised that way."
- "I don't have the stamina to entertain anymore, so how can I meet new people?"
- "What do I do about my insomnia and pain?"
- "I'm old. I'm not sure that all this is worth it."

The variety of issues that older adults face in treatment and recovery make a partnership between professionals, the patient, the family, and concerned persons essential to successful and considerate treatment and aftercare planning. The contribution of each team member is vital in developing a comprehensive plan that encourages the patient's sobriety and personal growth.

The Treatment Team as a Partner in Continuing Care

Because of the realities of aging, the transition from treatment to sober living is more difficult for older adults than it is for younger people. Older people usually have fewer sources of support due to the death of friends and loved ones and children who live far away. Older adults often have difficulty sharing problems and feelings due to values that stress stoicism and privacy. They may also have chronic medical problems that limit the kinds of activities in which they can participate. Treatment professionals need to modify their aftercare planning approach to take into account the unique needs and capabilities of each older adult. By doing so, traditional aftercare will expand into a more comprehensive concept of continuing care for older adults. It is only through this broader perspective that treatment professionals can set up their older adult patients for success.

The numerous and complex problems of treating the older

adult require treatment professionals to accept responsibility for comprehensive planning, and for tapping the resources of the team and community. While aftercare planning is usually the primary counselor's responsibility, the older adult's aftercare plan must be developed by a treatment team. Developing a plan that removes obstacles and provides opportunities for the older adult requires input from nursing and medical professionals, a physical therapist, a clergy member, and community agencies or other persons familiar with the older adult.

The Patient as a Partner in Continuing Care

Even the most comprehensive aftercare plan will be ineffective unless the patient follows it through. Priorities for most older adults center around the "Older Adult Agenda," which includes concerns about health care, finances, and personal independence. These concerns often overshadow the need for AA, counseling, or socialization. The aftercare team must determine the concerns of each older adult and engage him or her in the plans that impact his or her life. This means talking with each older adult about his or her concerns and fears, and carefully listening to what is and is not said. When this is done sincerely, the patient becomes an ally, and ambivalence or resistance is minimized.

Patient commitment to recovery is based on four critical issues.

- The patient recognizes his or her needs, capabilities, and limitations.
- The patient trusts that others understand and can help.
- The patient has a willingness to ask for and accept help.
- The patient has the motivation to recover.

While the general therapeutic milieu found in traditional chemical dependency treatment and the Twelve Steps of AA serves as a foundation, special older adult issues, and personal and cultural values, must also be addressed for them to make an investment in their recovery.

The Family as a Partner in Continuing Care

Family is a powerful influence in most older adults' lives. But the family is also deeply affected by a member's chemical abuse, and some members may have developed enabling behaviors to cope. Family members may feel angry or ashamed about their loved one's addiction. Or, they may feel burdened by and resistant to involvement in the recovery process. They may express ageist attitudes: "Let her drink, she's old." Or, "You can't teach an old dog new tricks." Family members will need support to process their own feelings, and the opportunity to understand how they have been affected by their family member's addiction. They will also need information about chemically dependent family systems and the importance of family recovery. This is true whether family members are active treatment team members, live far away, are emotionally distant, chemically dependent themselves, or if they have no relationship at all with the older adult.

The usual guidelines for family recovery are helpful when dealing with older adults' families, but they must be tailored to meet each older adult's and each family's specific needs. Recovery from chemical dependency means taking responsibility for one's self and making one's needs known. But how much assistance is appropriate for a chemically dependent older adult?

Older adults often have disabilities or limitations – including chronic medical problems, forgetfulness, or poor decision-making skills due to cognitive impairment – that prevent them from being completely independent. While independent in many areas, some older adults are unable to handle heavy household chores, financial decisions, or driving. In our society, family members typically step in to assist or take responsibility for some of these areas. Newly recovering older adults and their families often have difficulty sorting out who should be responsible for what. Family members may believe that the older adult's limitations are more severe than they truly are. Or, some older adults may believe it is the children's duty to take care of aging parents. Abilities may also be overestimated by older adults who value their independence and want to keep their troubles private, or by family members who feel overburdened with responsibilities.

Participation in creating an aftercare plan helps family members develop realistic expectations and navigate the fine line between support and policing the older adult. Because of the older adult's limitations and age, the family often vacillates between detaching and caregiving.

A discharge planning conference with the family and other concerned persons helps them become aware of what assistance is necessary and how community agencies and services can help meet the older adult's needs.

Chemical dependency professionals must encourage family members to realistically determine how much attention and involvement they can provide. Because they are often unsure of boundaries, and hopeful about continued sobriety after treatment, family members may overextend themselves, or make commitments that they cannot meet. Some family members may choose to be only minimally involved because of the history of their relationship with the older adult, fears of being vulnerable, or concerns about infringement on other parts of their lives.

COMPONENTS OF CONTINUING CARE

Continuing care for chemically dependent older adults must include attention to a variety of relevant issues, such as:

- health care concerns
- nonchemical coping mechanisms

- spirituality
- living situation
- housing options
- support for sobriety
- community resources

Most older adults will not need special planning in all these areas, but it is important to assess each area, since older adults may not be fully aware of their abilities and limitations.

Health Care Concerns

For some older adults, chemical abuse dulled chronic pain caused by injury or degenerative disease. Others found that alcohol or other drugs controlled their anxiety, insomnia, or depression. Some older adults' health is so precarious, and the effects of chemicals have been so debilitating, that resuming use may result in serious illness or even death. Whatever the circumstances, health care concerns should be carefully addressed as part of discharge planning.

Relationship with Physician

As people age, their health care issues multiply, as does their dependence on physicians. For some older adults, the same physician may have provided care for many years. For others, routine medical care is nonexistent: health crises are treated in the emergency room with little follow-up or monitoring. Many older adults have several doctors treating various conditions: an internist, a family practice physician, a cardiologist, and a psychiatrist, all of whom may be prescribing medications with or without the knowledge of other physicians' involvement.

Because older adults rarely obtain drugs illicitly, most of the drugs they abuse are prescribed. Compared with younger people, older adults use many more prescription and over-the-counter medications. Therefore, working with a physician who is knowledgeable about chemical dependency is critical to ensure appropriate medical care after treatment.

Ideally, one of the patient's physicians will be involved throughout the treatment process. But like family members of a chemically dependent person, physicians also get burned out and frustrated with difficult patients. It may be best to begin a new physician/patient relationship after treatment. When a number of physicians are involved, selecting a *coordinating physician* to oversee all aspects of health care is helpful. This physician can be regularly updated by the treatment team. These updates should include information about plans for maintaining the continuity of care with regard to both chemical dependency and aging issues. By making the coordinating physician a partner in the continuing care of an older adult, and by apprising him or her of nonmedical aspects of aftercare planning, such as living environment and ongoing counseling, the physician is better equipped to oversee the further administration of quality medical care.

Medication and Treatments

While medications are a fact of life for most older adults, many are uninformed or underinformed about how their medications affect their body and how they interact with other prescription and over-the-counter medications. Older adults are avid consumers of over-the-counter medications, and they often have the attitude that these drugs cannot be harmful because they can be bought without a prescription. Older adult patients must be made aware that many over-the-counter medications can be harmful—by themselves and when they interact with or potentiate prescription drugs.

Older adults need an understanding of how their medications work, their risks and benefits, and the importance of a consistent medication schedule. Some people, especially those newly committed to recovery, become fearful and view all medications as dangerous. Subsequently, they underuse their prescriptions. Patients must understand that, because of illness, some medications are essential to continued good health. An older adult's anxiety or reluctance to take medicines needs to be discussed with health care professionals before any changes are made.

One way to help patients acquire good medication practices while in primary treatment is to have them request their medication at appropriate times. Then, explain what the medication is, how it should be taken, and what the side effects or potential risks are. A patient's familiarization with a *daily dose system* will eliminate questions at home like "Did I take my noon dose?" Or, "How long ago did I take that medication?"

Cross tolerance should also be discussed prior to discharge. Few older adults are aware that the addictive process can be put into motion through use of mood-altering prescription medications. Handbooks, lectures, or lists of medications with potential for abuse can be useful in this regard.

Management of Chronic Health Problems

Alcohol and other abused drugs are toxins, and over time the body succumbs to their chemical assault. A large percentage of chemically dependent older adults have chronic health problems due to tobacco use; cigarette smoking and other chemical abuse seems to go hand in hand. Most chemically dependent older adults have at least one chronic health problem, and it is not unusual for a chemically dependent older adult to suffer from a number of chronic diseases. These may include:

- liver disease
- diabetes
- gastritis
- congestive heart disease
- emphysema
- peripheral neuropathy
- cerebellar degeneration

Many older adults enter treatment in a debilitated condition, and it is unclear if or how much they will improve. For these older adults, the first three to four weeks of abstinence is a time of restoration. While some or all symptoms of physical and cognitive impairment may abate or eventually disappear, chronic diseases will not disappear. Therefore, the patient and family must understand that, while symptoms can be treated, chronic disease cannot be cured. Patient education is an essential component in the management of chronic health conditions. Older adults often have little understanding of their medical problems and how they will affect their lifestyle.

For those with a disabling or terminal disease, support groups can be a source of continuing education and a place to express feelings associated with chronic illness. The I Can Cope groups offered by the American Cancer Society help people with a diagnosis of cancer. The American Lung Association has a support network for people with asthma, emphysema, and other lung diseases. Groups to support people with Alzheimer's disease and other dementias have mushroomed in the last few years, as has support and education for stroke survivors. Diabetes support groups also exist and have helped people of all ages manage their disease.

The need for ongoing attention to chronic illness issues should be discussed with the older adult during treatment. A referral to a community support group can be made prior to discharge, and it may be possible to have the older adult begin participation in a chronic illness support group before leaving treatment. This increases the likelihood that the older adult will continue to attend meetings after discharge.

It is not uncommon for older adults to also suffer from chronic mental health problems, especially depression. This makes continued monitoring and follow-up of an older adult's mental health another integral part of continuing care. Patients need and deserve to acquire information about mental health. Helping them gain knowledge about the signs and symptoms of mental illness, medications for treating it, and the importance of careful compliance with a prescribed drug regimen will help ensure that patients maintain good mental health after discharge.

Nutrition

As people age, their appetite decreases, their senses of taste and smell diminish, and they may not tolerate some nutritious foods. And while using alcohol and other drugs, some people eat very little, relying on alcohol's empty calories or nothing at all for sustenance. Others have a penchant for sweets, and snack on cookies and candies, leaving little appetite for more nourishing foods. Also, older persons with physical or cognitive impairments may be unable to safely prepare meals. All of these things can make proper nutrition more difficult for an older adult. The value of good nutrition and meal planning needs to be discussed with the patient during treatment, especially in cases where the patient needs to manage a chronic health care problem.

Many older adults do not enjoy eating alone, so they sometimes do not eat at all. Combining social stimulation with meals as a part of aftercare can be an ideal solution to this problem. Many senior centers offer dining where seniors can come to share in conversation and activities, and they usually have reasonable fees and can accommodate special diets. Some senior apartments also offer meals, usually in a social setting to foster regular interaction with others. For those who would rather be served in their home, Meals-on-Wheels is available through many local hospitals and health care centers. Volunteers deliver hot, nutritional meals, and as an additional benefit, the older adult receives a daily visit.

Exercise

Proper nutrition and exercise go hand in hand, but beginning an exercise program is difficult for older adults because of fears they might have. Many older adults believe that any exercise would be too strenuous for them, causing heart attacks or other medical problems. They are probably unfamiliar with

81

most modern exercise equipment and doubt that they are capable of using it. Also, many older adults are unaware of the emotional benefits of exercise–reduction of stress, anxiety, and depression. With encouragement and a physician's consent, an exercise program can begin during treatment and continue as part of aftercare.

Some senior centers offer exercise classes geared for older adults. These classes typically begin with simple stretching exercises and are great for older adults because they are able to meet other people and have fun while exercising. Classes often include members with a wide range of abilities and limitations–even those in wheelchairs can participate in many of the movements. Outside of senior center classes, exercise cycles, rowing machines, and treadmills can be used to build strength and endurance.

Walking is becoming known as the ideal cardiovascular exercise, and for many older adults it is the exercise of choice. In cold or stormy weather, mall walking has become popular. Older adults, singly or in groups, take advantage of the sprawling indoor space at shopping malls to get their exercise and to do a little window shopping.

Nonchemical Coping Mechanisms

Like their younger counterparts, many chemically dependent older adults have never developed, or have lost, nonchemical ways of coping with physical and emotional pain. Many have relied on alcohol or pills to numb unpleasant feelings. They may believe that to be strong, one must weather the storm and suffer through it.

As newly recovering people, older adults need to understand that old negative feelings and physical aches and pains will not magically disappear. And they need to understand that learning new behaviors and coping skills takes time. There may be times when things seem to change very slowly or not at all.

Learning to predict these times can help the older adult get through them without reaching for a drink or a pill.

Much work has been done in the area of relapse prevention in recent years, and the new knowledge that is coming from this research can be used to help older adults ask for help and form specific plans for how to reach out and to whom. Counselors should work with older adults before discharge to create a personal relapse prevention plan.

Self-indulgence is a concept that does not fit in many older adults' value systems. Instead, maxims like "better save for a rainy day" and "good people put themselves last" often determine how an older adult behaves. Self-nurturing, affirmation, and doing things just for fun can be powerful means of coping with pain without chemicals. It is important for older adults to give themselves permission to nurture themselves and get their needs met. Basic relaxation techniques can be very effective for older adults, especially if anxiety or insomnia are problems. Pain management, combined with the awareness that some aches and pains are part of growing older, helps older people get better in touch with their bodies and gain a sense of control over them.

Aftercare planning can include opportunities to further develop skills that promote self-esteem and personal satisfaction, which can help smooth the emotional ups and downs of early recovery. These skills will be particularly important as older adults encounter feelings of depression, anxiety, or self-pity.

Spirituality

Most older adults do not distinguish between organized religion and personal spirituality, so attention to this area is essential in aftercare planning. Older adults may feel deeply shameful or inadequate for not feeling closely connected to their Higher Power. Or, they may believe they are bad because they are angry with God due to an injustice or tragic event. These unresolved feelings may be decades old. Older adults may fear retribution if they express negative feelings toward God and religion.

Many older adults were raised believing that compliance with religious rituals and strict adherence to denominational rules are the keys to a satisfying spiritual life. Yet, they may not get satisfaction from these rituals and rules and probably do not feel free to explore other methods of spiritual expression.

Initiating a discussion of spirituality is the professional's responsibility, since few older adults readily identify this as an area of concern. These discussions can begin with one-on-one sessions and continue in group sessions focusing on spirituality. Treatment programming for older adults often includes participation in grief and loss groups. Exploration of grief and loss often helps older adults talk about their spiritual needs. Lectures and one-on-one sessions with clergy, as they complete the Fourth and Fifth Step, are also helpful for chemically dependent older adults.

Aftercare planning should include opportunities to continue spiritual growth. This may include religious participation, reading, daily meditation, or participation in sobriety support groups.

Living Situation

A living environment without adequate support is probably the greatest obstacle to recovery for older adults. If adequate support cannot be built into the current environment, a change is necessary.

Changing an older adult's living environment may seem drastic, but it is sometimes necessary to provide the older adult with the best opportunity to recover. The tendency for the patient and family members to deny the need for change must be addressed during treatment. Feelings about aging, coping with loss, dependence and independence, control, denial, role reversal, and fears about death will all need

exploration. Often, the patient and family know on an intellectual level that nursing assistance, supervision, and help with
the tasks of daily living are necessary, but the fantasy that
"Everything will be okay once I'm home" often persists. Discussions of the older adult's abilities and limitations, as well as
help processing feelings, are essential in gaining family support for a change in living environment.

An independent living skills evaluation and psychometric
testing can be used to determine appropriate housing. These
tools provide an objective measure of a patient's abilities and
limitations in an independent setting, and are useful as a start-
ing point to help patients and families deal with denial regarding constraints. An independent living skills evaluation as-
sesses a person's ability to perform basic tasks – organizing
and cooking a meal, using kitchen utensils safely, climbing
stairs, dressing and grooming, using the telephone, and
responding to an emergency situation. This evaluation can be
arranged through an occupational therapist or a similar evaluation can be developed by a treatment center's nursing staff.

Psychometric testing determines a patient's overall cognitive functioning. Brain damage caused by chemical abuse
tends to affect higher-level skills such as the ability to plan, an-
ticipate consequences, and weigh alternatives. Functioning on
visual/spacial tasks, such as driving and going up and down
stairs, may also be impaired by chemical abuse. But over-
learned tasks, such as writing checks, cooking, and language
skills, may remain intact.

Vulnerability to abuse or exploitation must also be assessed
prior to discharge. Older adults may be at risk because of cognitive impairment, poor judgment, or lack of assertiveness.
The aftercare team may need to explore financial safeguards
such as power of attorney and conservatorship to ensure ongoing monitoring and assistance. In a few cases, where the older
adult has severe, permanent disabilities, legal guardianship
may need to be considered.

Dedication to a recovering lifestyle can mean changes in familiar routines and environments. The family's and the counselor's sensitivity to this can contribute to an older adult's successful adjustment. For example, an older person who has structured his or her day around walking through the neighborhood and talking to friends along the way would have problems living in a high-rise next to a freeway where leisurely walks are not possible. A balcony with a pleasant view may be very important to an older adult who has traditionally sat on his or her porch and watched neighborhood activity each day.

The aftercare team must remember the enormous impact that a change in living environment has on an older adult. Older adults need time to consider and discuss their options, as well as time to explore their feelings. If the older adult's current environment is appropriate, but probably not adequate for the long-term, options for an eventual move may be discussed during aftercare planning. This gives the older adult a chance to consider alternatives and prepare for upcoming changes.

Housing Options

Own Home

Many older adults may be able to return to their own homes after treatment, particularly if a healthy spouse is at home or if children live nearby and can help with their care. The availability of comprehensive community support services can also make living in their own home appropriate for some older adults.

Home health services also allow many older adults to remain at home. Now, all but the most sophisticated services can be provided in a person's home. In addition, many home health agencies offer homemaker services. Homemakers keep the house neat, grocery shop, cook meals, run errands, and take the older person to appointments. Physical, occupational, and speech therapy can also be arranged in the home through many home health care agencies.

Adult day-care is an option for those with cognitive impairments, behavioral problems, or who have a working spouse or family member living with them. While the main caretaker goes to work or gets some private time, the older person is brought to a structured, individualized day-care program and returned home in the evening.

Home-Share programs are also available in many communities. In these programs, the older adult shares his or her home with a younger person. Each situation is unique and attempts are made to take each person's needs into account: some Home-Share partners receive free room and board in return for performing household chores; others are simply renters, and their reassuring presence is all the older adult needs.

Many community organizations offer low-cost maintenance services for older adults, such as raking, mowing, pruning, and shoveling. These services help older people keep up their homes and yards.

Senior Apartments

Moving from the family home to an apartment is an option for some older adults leaving treatment. For them, stairs at home may have become too difficult to navigate, or they may feel lonely in a large home that used to be filled with children and activity. Also, the family homestead may simply contain too many memories of bygone days or a deceased spouse. In recent years, more apartments are accepting pets, and this may be important to those for whom a dog or a cat is a cherished friend.

Some senior apartment complexes offer residents complete independence. Others offer a variety of health and home services and promote activity and social interaction. These services can usually be tailored to each older adult's needs. Some buildings offer emergency call systems along with daily "I'm okay" checks. Nearly all senior apartment complexes offer apartments designed for people with physical disabilities.

Contrary to popular belief, one older adult culture does not exist. Just as the older adult population is comprised of groups that differ in terms of lifestyle, interests, and expectations, the tone of each apartment complex varies. Some complexes support sobriety and may even offer on-site AA meetings. Some apartments tend to attract a young senior: fifty-five to sixty-five years old, often with a spouse, and who is active, enjoys traveling, recreation, and a fast-paced lifestyle. Others attract the older tenant who requires more support and medical care, and who enjoys a stable, slow routine.

While many senior apartments include a number of services and safety features, it is important to remember that apartment living is essentially independent, and is not a substitute for nursing care, behavior control, or constant supervision.

Board and Care

This option may be most appropriate for the older adult whose physical condition is fragile, who has mild to moderate cognitive impairment, psychiatric problems, or tenuous behavioral control. Board and care facilities are typically small and strive for a comfortable, home-like atmosphere. Structure, consistency, and individualized attention helps those unable to be completely independent get the support and assistance they need. Freedoms such as walks through the neighborhood and shopping can be retained based on an older adult's abilities. In these facilities, staff monitors compliance with a patient's aftercare plan, encouraging and sometimes ensuring that the older adult follows through.

Nursing Homes

Long-term care may be appropriate for those who require ongoing nursing or psychological care beyond what home health care can provide.

While many older adults, and society in general, hold a dim

view of nursing homes, a visit to a quality nursing home can go a long way in dispelling fears and misconceptions. Nursing homes are staffed with multidisciplinary teams designed to meet each resident's physical, emotional, social, and spiritual needs. Chemical dependency aftercare planning can be incorporated into the nursing home's plan of care, and, depending on the older adult's progress, may be a transitional step to a more independent living environment.

The decision for nursing home placement can be difficult for everyone involved. But when other options have been tried and found inadequate, long-term care in a nursing home is sometimes the only realistic alternative. Obtaining accurate information about nursing homes, and encouraging the older adult and family members to express their feelings, will help make a transition successful.

Nursing home staff are not typically trained in chemical dependency, and they may not realize that controlled drinking is not appropriate for the chemically dependent older adult. The dangers of *cross addiction* to mood-altering medications also needs to be discussed. Chemical dependency professionals can do their job by providing nursing home staff with clear and practical guidelines for aftercare.

Sobriety is the basis for recovery, and ongoing support for sobriety is important for chemically dependent older adults in nursing homes. While they may not be actively drinking, nursing home residents who are chemically dependent need continued support to process feelings, maintain self-esteem, and grow in recovery. It may be possible for the older adult to participate in AA or a chemical dependency aftercare group. In other situations, one-to-one visits, perhaps by AA members, and appropriate reading materials and audiotapes can help the older adult remain connected with and dedicated to recovery.

Support for Sobriety

AA Involvement

As is true for younger people, AA involvement is the cornerstone of recovery for older adults. There are, however, special issues that must be addressed to make AA participation accessible and rewarding for older adults.

Because many older adults have values that stress stoicism, independence, and keeping emotions private, sharing feelings and details of personal problems may feel uncomfortable. Moreover, older adults typically are not accustomed to admitting failures and difficulties because shame is especially acute among those who have viewed addiction as a personal weakness and moral problem.

Although older adults may be comfortable identifying themselves as chemically dependent in the controlled setting of a treatment center, it may be more difficult for them to admit this in public. Older adults may doubt the anonymity of AA meetings, or feel embarrassed and ashamed about their addiction. To make the transition from treatment to AA easier, it is helpful to have older adults attend outside AA meetings while still in treatment. Initial fears can then be dealt with in the therapeutic setting of the treatment center.

Like anyone else, older adults relate most easily to those with whom they share values, concerns, and lifestyles; it is much easier for them to develop a sense of community and belonging with other older adults. This is not to say that young recovering people and older recovering people cannot learn and grow together, but it is easier for older adults to begin recovery with others who are more similar to them than different.

Meeting time and location are important concerns for older adults. Because public transportation and volunteer drivers are available most frequently during the day, daytime meetings are preferred. Traditionally, AA meetings have been held in churches or similar settings that may not be accessible to persons who use a cane, walker, wheelchair, or who simply have trouble going up and down stairs. Adequate lighting is also important so that the older person can participate in readings and clearly see other group members. Having educational resources available and accessible is also important. For older adults with impaired sight, some AA books come in large print, and audiotapes are available for those who have difficulty reading.

Older adults may become involved at the local AA club, answering phones, greeting new members, and simply sharing their vast experiences and wisdom. They can be encouraged, in the tradition of AA, to reach out to other recovering people; to give and receive.

Sponsorship

Sponsors for recovering older adults are special people. Regardless of the sponsor's age, he or she must be sensitive to the older adult's values, issues, and feelings about aging. Sponsors must also be aware of their own attitudes about aging, disability, and their family of origin. As they make themselves aware of these things, sponsors may find themselves growing in unexpected ways. Although empathy, understanding, and patience are essential, the sponsor must be able to appropriately confront the older person and not accept excuses that hinder recovery. Like family members, sponsors must navigate the fine line between helping older adults take responsibility for themselves and accepting their limitations and problems due to aging.

It is important for older adults to understand that sponsors are not simply friends, but that they have a special role and responsibility. Older adults have responsibilities too.

- To be honest with their sponsor.
- To ask for help when it is genuinely needed.
- To share their feelings and concerns.

Beyond special concerns, general guidelines other people use for selecting a sponsor are applicable to older adults as well. Rapport, frankness, empathy, and sensitivity to the recovering person's situation and concerns are all characteristics of the effective sponsor. Above all, older adults must be comfortable enough with their sponsor to risk sharing their feelings, being vulnerable, and listening openly.

Working and Volunteering

All people need a sense of purpose, productiveness, and structure in their lives. These can be especially hard to come by for chemically dependent older adults who have isolated themselves, had little structure, or who have physical limitations due to aging or illness. Working or volunteering can provide these older adults with the opportunities they need to guard against feelings of low self-worth and negative attitudes.

Developing new interests or returning to previously satisfying endeavors must be discussed as part of aftercare planning. For some, this may mean returning to work. For others, reinvolvement in a previously held volunteer position is appropriate. Still others may try totally new activities. The chemical dependency professional needs to help the older adult understand the importance of structure and balance in early recovery, help them explore options, and provide feedback regarding the appropriateness of the older adult's plans. This is especially important because older adults are often unrealistic about their capabilities and needs. For example, an older person who worked part-time for a few years two decades ago may be hoping to find a full-time job immediately after treatment. Older persons with chronic medical problems may believe they are incapable of making any contribution to others or becoming involved in a hobby. Some who are retired after successful careers may think that because they are no longer "in the fast lane," their ideas are not as important. By helping them realistically assess the role of working or volunteering in recovery, the counselor can help older adult patients make positive lifestyle changes.

Some professionals are reluctant to promote volunteering among the newly recovering, but for older adults, the benefits of interaction with others, involvement in a cause, and the feeling of making a contribution that volunteering brings usually outweigh the risks to an older adult's recovery. Working and volunteering are a part of the balanced lifestyle that is so important to continued sobriety after treatment.

Prior to discharge from treatment, older adult patients should have specific information about activities they are interested in. Initial appointments or interviews can be set up soon after discharge. If an older adult is still employed, contact should be made with his or her employer to prepare for the return to work. When these important contacts have been made and appointments set up, older adults are more likely to follow through with and become involved in their aftercare plan.

Special Issue Groups

Most older adults have unresolved grief issues, including grief over the death of loved ones, lost usefulness and productivity, diminished physical capabilities, or lifestyle changes. As chemical dependency progresses, grief may not be recognized or dealt with in healthy ways. During recovery, these feelings surface and are often intense, even if the event that caused them happened many years ago. It is not uncommon for an older adult who lost a spouse decades ago to feel sadness and grief for the first time while in treatment.

As chemical dependency professionals, it is important to help older adult patients get in touch with their grief and find healthy ways to express it and other feelings. One-to-one sessions with a counselor or chaplain are a good place to start. Books and pamphlets about healthy ways to express feelings can give older adults information and support. One frequently used exercise to help a patient through grief is letter writing. Older adults may write a letter to a deceased loved one, sharing their feelings, saying what was left unsaid, and explaining the direction their life has taken since the death. Sharing this letter in a group of peers can be a powerful, moving, and healing experience. Support groups focusing specifically on grief can give older adults additional opportunities to work through these difficult feelings.

Male and female roles have changed dramatically in the past few decades, and many older adults feel conflict, ambivalence, and guilt about these changes. They may feel their values are under attack, or they may simply be unsure of what is appropriate behavior. As a result, assertiveness, intimacy, and self-image issues may need to be addressed. The need to further explore these issues as a part of ongoing recovery should be discussed prior to discharge from treatment.

Gender-segregated support groups can help older adults work through role changes and practice new behaviors. Daily readings on men's and women's issues and reading relevant books and pamphlets may also be useful.

Some older adults need to depend on others due to physical or cognitive disabilities. Like many other people, older adults may need guidance in striking a balance between asking for help and maintaining a healthy independence. Help may also be needed to change controlling, rigid, and manipulative behaviors, as well as to develop healthy relationships with their children.

Enabling behaviors may also be a problem. Enabling behaviors must be appropriately confronted throughout the treatment process, as well as addressed during aftercare planning. For example, some older adults may not think twice about doing laundry for a grown son who lives nearby. Or, they may be opposed to having another family member enter treatment because they do not want him or her to experience painful feelings. Yet, what younger people see as enabling is often social convention or a sign of concern and caring by older adults. To them, the idea of helping a loved one by "hurting" them is new.

Chemical dependency professionals must constantly, but gently, challenge these long-held beliefs and behaviors. They must help the older adult learn healthy beliefs and behaviors and find new ways to show they care. Some older adults gain insight by reading pertinent materials long after discharge from treatment. Recommending specific books, pamphlets, and tapes can encourage this. Ideally, older adults would receive some materials about these issues while they are still in treatment.

Older adults should be encouraged to discuss their thoughts and questions about these issues with peers in aftercare and AA, as well as to ask for support in changing their behaviors.

Community Resources

Local Support Networks

Most communities have or are developing support networks for seniors. The local senior center and area agencies that work with older adults can help the treatment team tap into available services. Area churches are often a large part of the local support network and can also help treatment professionals find services for older adults. Veterans groups provide a wide range of help to older adults who qualify, and can also assist in setting up and implementing aftercare plans.

Senior centers are often the hub of the local service network, and are clearing-houses for information about available services. Senior center staff are usually well-informed about available services and can assist the treatment team in accessing them, often providing basic information and assistance in cutting the red tape that can sometimes be a barrier to obtaining some services.

Because many recovering older adults need services in a variety of areas, chemical dependency aftercare plans can become complex and cumbersome. For example, it may be difficult or impossible for an older adult to remember when the home health care worker comes . . . when to be at the senior center . . . which day their doctor appointment is . . . and how they are getting to the AA meeting. Clarity and simplicity are essential in helping the older adult follow through with an aftercare plan.

Anything that helps simplify an aftercare plan is useful. Using an older adult's personal techniques for organizing "things to do" is best. For some, a calendar with appointments and transportation arrangements filled in is effective. Others may prefer to organize their time from a copy of the aftercare plan that specifies services, contact persons, phone numbers, and appointments. Still others may want each appointment listed on a separate note card that they can hang on the refrigerator as a reminder of the day's activities. Whatever technique is used, it is important that the older adult understand and know how to use the format. Related information about appointments, such as transportation, cost, and materials to bring along should be included with each notation of appointment dates and times.

Some older adults need help remembering and planning for appointments. Family members may be able to assist. Or, community agency personnel, such as a home health care aide, a public health nurse, or a county social worker can help. Ideally, one person or agency should be aware of all services provided, monitor the older adult's response and changing needs, and address any problems that develop. Although this often means a large commitment of time and money, many serious problems can be avoided or dealt with early on, perhaps preventing medical complications, relapse, or other consequences of inadequate support.

Transportation

Getting around is relatively simple for most people. They get in their cars and go where they need to. When problems arise, many people can usually rely on friends or public transportation. But for older adults, getting around is often more difficult. Some older adults may be unable or unwilling to drive at night, during winter or stormy weather, or on freeways and expressways. A bout with illness or an injury may also prevent an older adult from driving. Cognitive impairment, lack of money – all of these problems force many older adults to depend on others for transportation.

It is important for treatment professionals to understand the frustrations transportation problems present. Friends and relatives have busy lives, and the older adult may be reluctant to impose on them. Walking to the bus stop may be difficult, or even dangerous for some older adults. Taxi services are often too expensive. For older adults with physical disabilities, special vehicles may have to be reserved. This often needs to be done days ahead and long waits are common.

Combining resources may be a solution. Senior center transportation services, combined with other services available through churches, hospitals, friends, and relatives can usually meet an older adult's transportation needs.

Socialization and Recreation

When older adults retire or go through other dramatic life changes, they sometimes become isolated and lose the structure, human contact, and feelings of productiveness that are essential to personal growth. Restoring opportunities for socialization and rewarding work and recreation is an integral part of aftercare planning.

Older adults often have many useful skills and a lot of time on their hands. Senior centers and other organizations can help older adult's put their skills to work. For some, taking a class, earning a degree, or returning to work may be realistic possibilities. For others, interests in old hobbies and new pursuits may develop as recovery begins and become satisfying. Many clubs and groups welcome older adults as members. Programs like Foster Grandparents may be a good way for some older adults to give, receive, and develop feelings of connectedness to others. The key to an effective socialization and

97

recreation plan is to involve older adults in the creation of it so that they can include activities that are meaningful and rewarding to them.

❋ ❋ ❋ ❋ ❋

Developing and implementing a comprehensive aftercare plan for older adults challenges the treatment team. Some people may believe that the time, energy, and expense required to meet older adult's needs is prohibitive. But if the treatment team is made up of professionals with different areas of expertise and a multitude of skills, the task is not as overwhelming.

Developing resources and a support network for recovering older adults is a process, just as recovery is a process. Each time a treatment team goes through the aftercare planning process for an older adult, new information is discovered, new community contacts are made, and the team's effectiveness is enhanced. In the process, awareness of recovering older adults is heightened and sensitivity to their needs increased.

Because sober older adults can and do contribute to their families, society, and the work force, treatment professionals must develop comprehensive aftercare plans to provide the best chance of continued recovery. Through these efforts, treatment professionals affirm the value and dignity of all people.

To me, old age is always fifteen years older than I am.

– Bernard M. Baruch

CHAPTER FIVE

FAMILY ISSUES

Bobbie Walker

The families of older adults with alcohol or other drug problems are as different from each other as are the individual older adults. Each family is the product of interactions among its members over their entire history, which includes shared joy, sorrow, celebration, and grief. Each family develops its own myths and secrets, and its own patterns of sharing and avoidance. Families of chemically dependent older adults often have the same problems that trouble normal families, yet these problems are most likely exacerbated by the older adult's addiction. In addition to the problems addiction poses to the family, each family member must also learn to cope with the problems of aging. And, in the case of early-onset addiction, long-standing patterns of unhealthy coping behaviors need to be unlearned.

Just as each family is unique, each family member has developed his or her own method of coping that helped him or her to survive in the family. It is important for counselors and treatment staff to recognize that each family and each family member is doing the best they can to deal with the issues of chemical dependency and aging.

In counseling, each family member will need to find his or her own solutions to problems—solutions he or she must own and act on if they are to be effective. Solutions that work for one person, or one family, may not work for others.

FAMILY NEEDS

Each family dealing with chemical dependency has unique concerns that need to be identified and addressed by the treatment staff. Families of older chemically dependent persons have the added problem of dealing with aging, chronic illness, grief and loss, and family responsibility for the older adult.

The family of a chemically dependent older adult sometimes has a different makeup than the traditional family. His or her children, who are now adults, may or may not be involved in family affairs; they may be cut off emotionally or geographically. Spouses may have died, divorced, or remarried. In some cases, the family may be a best friend, a neighbor, or extended relatives. Or, there may be no one.

Validation

The primary need of family members is *validation*. They need to be understood and accepted as a family that has functioned as best it could under the circumstances. Along the way, family members may have been criticized, judged, and shamed by well-meaning but misguided friends and relatives. Now, they need to know that the treatment staff acknowledges their attempts to cope as the best they could manage under the circumstances. And they need recognition for having the courage to seek help.

They need to be recognized for their strength, effort, and deep feelings of anger, rage, frustration, exasperation, fear, rejection, hopelessness, concern, and love.

Stabilization

Along with validation, family members of chemically dependent older adults need *stabilization*. They need to understand that the enemy is not Dad or Grandma, but alcohol and other drugs, and that the conflict is between the family and the addiction, not between the family and the addicted member.

Some family members of chemically dependent older adults have never learned to trust. They will look for or create reasons not to trust the staff, other family members, or the treatment program. There are many factors that keep family members from trusting. One is the fact that family members may not have shared personal problems with each other and were taught "rugged individualism." Another is a tendency in some families to distrust any counseling except that which comes from doctors or clergy. Shame can also impact trust. Counselors need to avoid reinforcing this distrust by providing accurate information, promising only what can be done, and by being trustworthy. When counselors make mistakes, they must acknowledge them openly, and to the best of their ability, rectify them. Some family members may look to counselors as experts and the family's savior. This trap can be avoided if counselors are honest about their role in the treatment process and are trustworthy.

It may take more time to work with the extended, and possibly alienated, family of a chemically dependent older adult than it does to work with families of younger chemically dependent people. During the discharge and aftercare planning process, the staff must help the family with many details unique to older adults. And because some chemically dependent older people have been abusing alcohol and other drugs for decades, family members often need more time and encouragement to establish trust in the process of recovery in their lives, and in the life of the older adult.

Education

Education about addiction and recovery is another great need for families of older adult abusers. In addition to understanding addiction and recovery, they will need to learn what the normal problems of aging are, and how these are affected by chemical abuse.

Since older adults tend to take more prescription and over-the-counter drugs than younger people, family members will need to learn how these medications interact with alcohol and the other drugs the older adult may take. They will need to know which behavioral changes might be due to normal aging and which could be due to alcohol or other drugs. For family members who are involved in the older adult's aftercare program, education about medical problems, nutrition, exercise, and socialization are very important, as is information about available community resources to help the older adult and the family. The treatment staff needs to be knowledgeable about senior centers, day care services, veterans benefits, caretaker support groups, cancer support groups, grief groups, and other support services for older adults and their families.

Loss and grief counseling is also especially important to families of chemically dependent older adults. All families have to deal with loss, but for the family of the early-onset older alcoholic, grief can be complicated by deep feelings of anger, guilt, abandonment, resentment, neglect, and shame. Spouses of older adult alcoholics may feel grief over the destruction of their marriage relationship, over lost retirement dreams, lost respect for their partner, and missed opportunities for themselves. And they may feel grief over having been depressed so often. Grown children may feel grief over the loss of their parent to alcoholism and over missed opportunities. Teaching family members about the grieving process, and giving them permission to grieve and express other feelings, is a valuable tool they can use later as they deal with other grief issues, such as separation from loved ones, or a loved one's illness or death.

Counseling

Helping family members become familiar with the objectives of addiction counseling, including family counseling, will help make communication between the counselor and the family clear. Some issues are best handled in a family program, if a family program is available. These issues may include

- an impending separation or a divorce in a fifty-year marriage.
- an adult child struggling with how to support both parents in recovery.
- an ailing or angry spouse agonizing over his or her ability to care for a chronically ill and recovering mate.

While these situations may not sound too unusual to professionals who counsel family members, support in dealing with these issues is crucial for the family members of an early-onset abuser, especially for the spouse. When crises occur, and his or her strength is low, the spouse of a chemically dependent older adult needs extra time to recover. She or he must be given support, encouragement, time to heal, and time to learn new ideas and coping strategies. Counselors need to always support the spouse's self-esteem, and then work to increase its strength.

Just as it takes longer for a chemically dependent older adult to benefit from treatment, it often takes longer for family members of a chemically dependent older adult to recognize their own feelings about the family situation and their relationship with the addicted person. Repetition of educational information can help them accept their feelings and their experience in the family. Saying things such as "You must be very tired of working so hard for so many years to make him stop drinking," and "You don't have to decide anything right now; you have time," or "You needn't do anything until you are ready" will validate family members' feelings and give them time to think before they act.

As a result of family counseling, individual members may recognize the need for additional individual help in some areas. Long-denied needs for self-expression and fulfillment frequently emerge from these sessions, allowing the individual to once again pursue personal fulfillment.

COUNSELING INDIVIDUAL FAMILY MEMBERS

For many aging couples, the last fourth of their lives is a time to relax and enjoy the fruits of the work from the first three-fourths of their lives. Retirement brings time and energy to do things long planned for – travel, leisure activities, pursuit of old hobbies and interests, and the development of new ones. Many healthy seniors also volunteer generous amounts of time and energy to various causes. With both the husband and the wife at home, the relationship may require some redefinition. And although this can be a problem for some couples, for most it is a time of renewed sharing and enjoyment. Health problems are common for older couples, yet they need not overshadow the quiet pleasures of these later years. Their children have grown and are usually busy with their own lives. Older adults may have new and special relationships with their grandchildren. And while their children tend to be involved with their own families, they are usually helpful and supportive to the degree that their parents' need.

Contrast this happy vision of retirement and aging with the reality of how an early- or late-onset alcoholic experiences retirement and aging: spouses are often emotionally cut off from their partner and other family members, and have probably developed controlling or dominating behaviors, or become passive and depressed. Feelings of hopelessness and helplessness build around the passive spouse. Overall, spousal relationships are nonexistent at worst and strained at best. Emotional support is usually a thing of the distant past. Adult children may have cut off relations with the addicted parent or refuse to bring grandchildren over for visits. Adult children may have also suffered greatly from intimacy and relationship problems with their own spouses and children because of their unmet needs as a child of a chemically dependent parent.

Characteristics of the Spouse of an Early-Onset Alcoholic

In the case of early-onset alcoholism, the spouse, who, in this age group, is most often female, is probably in her fifties, sixties, or seventies, and shares many of the characteristics of other women in her age group. Her cultural expectations include being a good housewife, mother, and caretaker. She expects to depend on her husband for financial support. She lets him set the tone and direction of family life; he makes the large decisions—where to live, what to buy, and controls the finances.

While many females of this age have worked outside the home, their main occupation is housewife. For many of these women, divorce is the absolute last option, and most refuse to consider it. There are cultural, religious, financial, and self-esteem reasons for this. Women of this age often have no money of their own, and they know that joining the work force will earn them only a meager living. The self-esteem of many of these women is tied to their husbands' self-esteem, which has a disastrous effect when he has a drug problem. These women may think that it is better to be a "wife" than a "nothing."

A woman's status in these families was usually tied to her children and husband. Whether a woman was independent or passive, she was expected by those around her to accept her husband's authority. For the female spouse of a chronic alcoholic, this often meant living for many years in a highly stressful situation where emotional and financial support was unpredictable or nonexistent. The husband coming home drunk or not at all probably led to many years of chilly silences or late-night arguments. Still, many women felt a duty to fulfill their housewife role, so they would continue to cook and clean for this person, growing more angry, empty, and lonely. These women lived with the fear of others finding out about their husbands' drinking, so they may have isolated themselves socially to prevent other people from discovering their secret.

Female spouses from this generation often feel a responsibility to maintain the status quo in their family. After years of adjusting, coping, arguing, and caretaking, she may begin to realize that her efforts are not causing her husband to quit drinking or making family life more harmonious. Consequently, she may feel that her life has been wasted, that all of her efforts have been fruitless. She may feel like a failure because she could not make her husband quit drinking. This despair is real and intense.

Alice and Tom's Story

Alice, sixty-three, was attending the family program with her husband Tom, who was in treatment for alcoholism. She had been a full-time homemaker during their forty-three years of marriage, and although Tom worked regularly, he was also a regular, practicing alcoholic. Alice looked very depressed. Her head hung down, and she rarely made eye contact. Her voice was weak, and her demeanor said: "What I say and think counts for nothing." She was forgetful, distracted, and gave the appearance of being mentally slow. Indeed, the treatment staff wondered if she was suffering from the early stages of mental decline. She certainly was very depressed.

She was quite surprised and shocked when told of the staff's concerns about her mental ability, and she began to make greater efforts for her own sake. With counseling, education, goal setting, and the support of her daughters, Alice began volunteering in her community and socializing with friends, visiting them and inviting them over for coffee. She began to understand more about chemical dependency and how she could help herself. She enjoyed learning how to make new choices for herself and developing a life of her own. She was eventually able to tell Tom that she would no longer put up with his drinking behaviors.

Denial can be very strong in spouses of chemically dependent older adults—especially female spouses. Some spouses deny alcohol problems for decades, even denying that alcohol abuse is harmful. Some may consider abusive drinking normal. Perhaps in their childhood, their parents or relatives drank abusively. Many older adults have little understanding of alcoholism or other drug dependency. They picture the alcoholic as a stumbling drunk or skid-row bum. They tend to view alcoholism as a moral issue, and never go beyond this archaic myth. Even when this myth is challenged by their own experience, the stigma remains for many. Gently reminding older people of the facts can help counselors wear away this myth.

In addition to education about alcoholism and other drug dependence, the female spouse of an older chemically dependent person needs to learn about aging's affect on the body, and the health needs of her spouse. She also needs to understand the affects of alcohol on the older body, and how alcohol interacts with medications, prescription and over-the-counter. Teaching her this will require patience and repetition. Older spouses can be able learners, but old beliefs, denial, and rationalizations have been a part of their behavior for a long time, and will take a while to be replaced.

The female spouse of an older chemically dependent person may become a *reactor*—a person who reacts to the behavior of the drinking spouse by becoming confused, unsure of herself and her actions. She may go along with the wishes of the drinker, and feel powerless to resist. This person often loses hope, believing her partner will drink forever and that her personal needs will never be met. This method of coping leads to depression, loss of vitality, extreme sadness, and feelings of victimization. Alice was a reactor.

Or, the female spouse may become an *initiator*—a person who always tries to make the drinker behave. The initiator may deny that alcohol is a problem. Or, they may try to make the drinker change his drinking behavior. Her goal is to change the behavior of the person who drinks, not necessarily to stop the drinking.

The initiator usually appears to be a strong, controlling, take charge type of person. She may feel burdened, tired, angry, and punish the drinking spouse. Or, she may transfer those feelings into compulsive behaviors such as fussiness, tidiness, or perfectionism.

Sue and Tim's Story

Sue worked as a switchboard receptionist for a group of insurance salespeople. She handled messages for thirty-five salespeople and loved her job. She typically worked fifty to sixty hours a week and could not take off from work to come to family counseling. Her relationship with Tim, her sixty-year-old husband, was emotionally distant, and she felt in charge of what happened to him and to them. She looked nervous, with her hands and face constantly moving. Sue was bright and very capable of making decisions. Tim had been in treatment many times before and seemed to have a mild form of alcoholic dementia. He lived with the idea that he was a high-caliber professional, although he had not worked in any capacity for five years.

Sue was difficult to work with because she knew all the intellectual answers. Still, she was so set in her initiator role that she could not imagine not being a caretaker of her husband. While she was polite and

110

listened to professional opinions, she discounted them and went her own way. The first effort to reach Sue was made by identifying with her efforts to make everything work well, to empathize with her by saying: "You have worked really hard to try to make your husband well and your life happy; you must be very tired and lonely." She began to respond to this approach by recognizing her own pain, but she never got beyond this point. Unfortunately, Sue decided to have her husband return with her to their small apartment, and she stopped seeking help for herself. Her need to control her husband and rely on herself was too great.

Another way a female spouse may cope is by *detaching*. This spouse may have emotionally cut herself off from her marriage, going on with life without her husband. She may say she is concerned about her spouse, but take no action to help him. She may turn a blind eye to his chemical abuse, going so far as to ignore serious physical problems.

And serious physical problems do develop in chemically dependent older adults. After years of attempting to control his drinking, the older alcoholic may give up hope of ever quitting, so he decides to give in to it. He says: *I am alcoholic, and I cannot quit, so why try.* This is also true for the spouse who says: *I have tried and tried to make this person stop drinking and behave, and I cannot, so why try. I give up on his drinking. I am defeated.* At this point, the spouse often decides to live her life with a drinking husband, her emotions are set, and life becomes manageable just as it is. In fact, the husband must continue drinking for things to remain the same. Unconsciously, the spouse works to keep things the same because she knows how to manage this way.

Ann and Jim's Story

> *Jim, a long-time alcoholic, was in outpatient treatment and his spouse and daughter were in family ther-*

apy. One day, Jim had gotten very drunk and fell on the floor of his garage and couldn't get up. His wife, Ann, worked as a secretary. She went to work each day for three days, walking around her husband on the garage floor. Only when their daughter came in and saw her father on the floor was Jim taken to the hospital. Jim was in the hospital for a month, in a nursing home for two months, and then was moved into inpatient treatment.

How could Ann have left her husband on the garage floor for three days without helping him? Was she awful for not helping him? In the past, Ann had taken Jim to the hospital many times. She had dragged him to bed many times, and had cleaned up his diarrhea many times. Ann lost hope and cut herself off from Jim's problems. She did not see that Jim needed medical attention. To her, she was just ignoring one more bout of excessive drinking.

Many female spouses react in similar ways. They have lived through hellish experiences, not getting their own needs met by their husbands. So, to survive, they may sever the emotional attachment they once had to their husbands and begin accepting the status quo to make their lives manageable.

Clearly, Ann's, Sue's, and Alice's coping methods were not helpful to them or their spouses, and were built on false assumptions. Yet, it is important that counselors not punish, reject, or criticize female spouses of chemically dependent older adults for ways they coped. The counselor's job is to empathize with their efforts, and then to educate and nurture them into more appropriate and healthy coping methods.

Before effective therapeutic work can begin, a connection must be made between the spouse and the counselor. By empathizing with her, by listening to her and hearing her pain, the counselor can begin to make this connection. Saying things that show understanding, such as, "That must hurt very much," "What's it like to be the breadwinner and the caretaker at the same time?" "How did you get your needs met?" and "Who was there for you?" will help the spouse gain trust in the counselor and the therapeutic process. When the spouse trusts, she knows that the counselor understands her anguish and acknowledges her attempts to solve her husband's drinking.

As the counseling relationship develops, the spouse needs to understand that the results of her efforts have not been helpful to herself or her husband. Then, she may be ready to consider new ways of dealing with the problem. Educating her about alcoholism, using her husband to show how the disease affects a person, and explaining the need for her own mental and physical health, will help her consider new ways of dealing with the problem.

Older adults have lived many years and have gained important knowledge and experience. Many have risen above crises they had when they were younger and gained some deep understandings about life. The counselor's job is to tap into these strengths. In some ways, older female spouses catch on quickly when they feel validated, stabilized, encouraged, and are aware of their options.

Characteristics of the Spouse
Of the Late-Onset Alcoholic

The female spouse of a late-onset alcoholic usually has more experience with successful coping behaviors, and a healthy, fulfilling lifestyle. Her spouse's drinking or other drug abuse may develop gradually, or suddenly, as a response to retirement, a loved one's death, illness, or another loss. Or, he may have been a heavy, periodic drinker, but then, for some reason, the drinking becomes more regular.

The spouse may ignore or misinterpret the change in drinking or other drug abuse and not recognize that her partner needs help. Or, she may allow abusive drinking as a reaction to grief and think it will pass. So, the problem goes unattended, denied, ignored, and the family continues to function as if there was no problem, until some critical event—perhaps illness or accident—thrusts it into their awareness. A physician will notice symptoms of alcoholism and recommend that the family seek help. Recognition of the problem and referral to a suitable treatment source is crucial at this time. Loneliness, isolation, and grief are powerful issues for late-onset alcoholics. Many are divorced or widowed, and their children often do not recognize or have time for a parent's problems.

Lack of education is the most significant issue for the spouse and other family members of a late-onset alcoholic. When the family gets accurate information and guidance, their strengths come forth and they are able to get help for the afflicted member and themselves.

If abusive drinking or other drug abuse of a late-onset alcoholic continues for several years, the problems can become more severe, and will become similar to the problems of the early-onset alcoholic. As with the early-onset alcoholic, permanent physical and emotional damage can result.

Characteristics of the Male Spouse

Much of what has been written about the female spouse can also be applied to the male when his wife is the alcoholic or drug abuser. Some things are different though. For example, women are more likely than men to have problems with prescription drug addiction, and confusion may be the first reaction of their spouse. He may wonder: *Why is she acting this way?* Later, when the drug abuse is recognized and acknowledged, his feelings may change to frustration with the doctor because he or she prescribed it, and anger toward his spouse.

Like older women, older males also share behaviors, attitudes, and values with others of their generation. Most often, they have been the family provider and protector. Older men tend to be practical, logical, and concrete in their problem solving. Their solutions are action oriented: "Don't just stand there, do something!" Talking about feelings and needs may be uncomfortable and alien to them.

As with younger males in chemically dependent relationships, older males are more likely to leave a marriage than are female spouses. Those who stay in the marriage may have cut themselves off emotionally from their spouse or become over-involved in work or hobbies. Some deny, protect, and excuse their wife's behavior. One counselor was called in by a daughter to help the family intervene in the drinking of her seventy-two-year old mother. The counselor discovered that the daughter had known about her mother's excessive drinking for many years, but her father denied the problem and refused to seek help for his alcoholic wife. Only after the father died was the daughter able to intervene. Now, her mother is sober.

Needless to say, women are not the only caretakers and ena-blers. Some men, who feel confused by their wives' excessive drinking, become enabling and permissive about their wives' behavior. Overall, older men seem to have more difficulty than women acknowledging their own problems and feelings. Older men may also have difficulty participating in groups composed mostly of women. One-to-one counseling may be more helpful for them.

THE FAMILY AND AGING ISSUES

The picture described earlier of a happy, healthy family go-ing through the aging process – enjoying retirement, having time for traveling, hobbies, and grandchildren – can be true for many older adults. Yet, the older a person becomes, the more susceptible he or she is to medical, emotional, and financial problems. When medical problems arise for an older person, the healthier spouse typically takes over more of the family tasks, and the children may come in occasionally to help. Older adults who have Alzheimer's disease or another cognitive impairing illness usually learn, with their families, positive ways of coping. But when alcoholism and other drug abuse enters this picture, it confuses and compounds aging issues for everyone involved.

Brain Damage

When older adults abuse alcohol and other drugs, mental decline can happen dramatically fast, and can become permanent. A chemically dependent person's brain damage from long-term or short-term alcohol abuse affects all family members. The two questions for staff to answer are: (1) Is the brain damage organic or caused by alcohol or other drug abuse? (2) Is it temporary or permanent? Yet, these are difficult questions to answer; it is hard to define the nature of a person's cognitive impairment. Dealing with this is doubly hard for family members.

Family members need to be educated about the medical aspects of brain damage and taught how to deal with an older adult's mental decline. Family members often misinterpret symptoms of brain damage; they are familiar with the older adult's drinking behaviors and assume that signs of mental decline are a part of the addiction. Or, they see the mental decline as a result of aging, and may want to put their parent in a nursing home. Families are usually unaware that abstinence can improve the cognitive ability of an addicted person. In treatment programs, counselors commonly see patients whose family members and care providers recognized the possibilities of mental recovery. Yet, many other chemically dependent older adults are at home or in institutions because people did not recognize the possibilities for recovery.

Recovery from delusion – which is temporary – and dementia – which is permanent – may take, one, two, six or twelve months, depending on the severity of the damage. To adjust to permanent damage, the brain can form new pathways that take over damaged areas of mental functioning.

116

Recovering from permanent or temporary brain damage requires abstinence, good food, physical exercise, social stimulation, and self-esteem building. Some older adults may need a protected, supportive environment for the rest of their life, while others become capable of functioning on their own.

Family members are often confused by the older person's confabulation, which is making up stories to fit remembered facts. Family members sometimes become angry and abusive because they think the person is lying.

Harold's Story

> *Harold, seventy-seven, remembers sitting at the table for dinner. He told his son this story: "Your mother called me to dinner; I came and sat down, but she never served dinner and I didn't get any food that night. She said the neighbor needed help, so she left me for the evening." The reality was that Harry was called to dinner, he came, but never touched his food. His wife encouraged him to eat, but he would not. Later, she cleaned up the kitchen and started knitting.*

Harold's story was not the result of a blackout or denial; it is a coping method used by people with Alzheimer's disease, alcohol dementia, and other cognitive impairing illnesses. They are not deliberately trying to deceive, but are filling in gaps in their memory with a story that makes sense to them. Once confabulation is recognized, then counselors and family members can stop becoming upset with the older adult and accept the reality of brain damage.

Dementia from alcohol, alcohol amnesic disorder, Korsakoff's syndrome, depression, poor nutrition, lack of social and mental stimulation—each of these can play a role in reducing the cognitive level of older adult drinkers. Family members typically need a lot of information about the effects chemical abuse has had on their family member. Treatment staff must be honest with them about the prognosis for cognitive

117

recovery. Often, no one knows how much recovery is possible from brain damage. Only time will tell.

Health problems for the older chemically dependent person are usually much more severe than health problems for older adults who are not chemically dependent. The incidence of strokes, diabetes, cardiovascular disease, cirrhosis of the liver, cancer, emphysema, and other disabling diseases is much higher in older adult alcoholics than in other older adults. If an older alcoholic becomes disabled by a health problem, his or her spouse is very likely to become a hostage to the caretaker role, unless they have received counseling about healthy ways to cope with the caretaker role. This spouse will benefit from participation in family counseling, Al-Anon, and a caregivers support group, along with education from services that teach people how to care for the aging.

Counselors can help the spouse and family members by talking with them about healthy caregiving. Caregivers must learn how to take time for themselves—by taking a day off, or asking another family member to take over. The family needs to learn to balance the needs of the disabled older adult with the needs of the rest of the family.

Agnes and Fred's Story

Agnes, a fifty-seven-year-old woman, was married to Fred, a sixty-eight-year-old chronic alcoholic. For both, this was their second marriage. They had met when Fred owned a supper club and Agnes came to work as his office manager. After ten years of marriage, they sold the club and retired. Fred was sixty-two and Agnes fifty-one. Although Fred had a long history of heavy drinking, he was never considered an alcoholic by those who knew him because he was a successful businessman.

Six years later, Fred was admitted to the local hospital for confusion, memory loss, and swollen legs and

118

feet. His secondary diagnosis was chronic alcoholism. Although his medical condition stabilized, he showed no improvement in his mental functioning. After being detoxified, he began exhibiting radical mood swings between deep depression and rage. His rage seemed to be triggered by Agnes' visits. He accused her of stealing his money, of being unfaithful, and he made other irrational and unfounded statements.

The hospital staff recommended that Fred not return to their home, but be placed in a long-term care facility for psychiatric patients. As Agnes contemplated this decision, she was torn between feelings of relief and guilt. Fred accused her of railroading him into an institution, and this thought was repulsive to her. Yet, she realized that if she was to have any peace and enjoyment in her life, she could not become Fred's caregiver during his remaining years. After several weeks of contemplation, she decided to follow the advice of the hospital staff, against the wishes of Fred and his family. Fred was transferred to a nearby facility for veterans, where she could visit him regularly. He is able to have home visits when his condition permits. Agnes has begun to develop a more independent and rewarding life for herself.

When death comes to a chemically dependent older adult, his or her spouse may feel a mixture of relief, guilt, and loss. If the surviving spouse has devoted a lot of time and energy to caring for the alcoholic, he or she will need to reorganize his or her life. Some spouses adjust very well after a normal period of grieving. Others need long-term help from a counselor, clergy, and friends. For still others, the adjustment is overwhelming and their lives are spent in loneliness, depression, and despair. A few are so relieved that they quickly move on to pursue their own plans.

Sometimes, the stress of years of living with an alcoholic

takes its toll on the nonalcoholic partner. He or she may die of stroke, cancer, heart attack, or another stress-related illness. This leaves the aging alcoholic alone, with no caretaker or companion. Unless the family or community services intervene, he or she is likely to drink more and follow his or her partner in death. If not, this person may end up in the service provider network, which takes on some of the roles of the family when the family is unable to care for them.

Adult Children

Children of chemically dependent older adults, because they grew up with chemical dependency in their families, may continue to practice, long into their adult lives, unhealthy behaviors they learned in their childhood. To cope with their parents' addiction, these children develop many different coping behaviors, including denial, caretaking, and rage, and being blaming, judgmental, critical, and intolerant. They are frequently untrusting, fearful, and emotionally distant. Adult children may hate their drinking parents, or be overly sympathetic toward them. They may feel both resentment and pity. Often, they are still enmeshed in the family system, but some are only peripherally involved. Others are completely cut off from the alcoholic parent and the rest of the family.

Shame is a common problem for children who grow up in an alcoholic or otherwise dysfunctional family, but shame is an even greater problem for children who grow up in homes where a parent's drug abuse is kept secret for many years. Shame lowers self-esteem and reduces a child's ability to develop self-responsibility. Because shame prohibits people from trusting their own sense of self-worth, it causes people to evaluate their worth in terms of how others view them. Children who feel shameful may swing between extremes— between blaming everyone and accepting everyone's blame; between being overly aggressive and defensive; between being overly passive and overly sensitive to others' criticism.

120

To shameful people, innocent remarks can be perceived as criticism, causing the shameful person to physically or emotionally withdraw. One man, whose mother was in treatment for alcoholism, came to a family group session for the first time. He was emotionally moved by the lecture, and he shared parts of his painful story, with tears running down his cheeks. The group leader, a counselor in the treatment program, realizing that self-disclosure was inappropriate at this stage in the group, attempted to redirect the group's attention back to the topic of discussion. Afterward, she talked to the man about his feelings and about continuing with the group. She also offered him individual counseling if that was his preference. As feared, he did not return to subsequent group sessions, nor did he call for an individual appointment. As a follow-up, he was called by the counselor, but he turned down invitations to come in for either group or individual participation in the program. The shame triggered by his self-disclosure was too powerful, and he could no longer face the group or the counselor.

Grown children of older adult alcoholics seem to be at one or the other extreme along the responsibility continuum. Some are rigid and super responsible, others are irresponsible, passive, and avoidant. Normal, healthy adjustment requires a balance along this line–a balance between responsibility to self and to others; between criticism and support and nurture; between following and leading; between giving and taking; and between working and playing. It is holding on to the self, even when in a sharing relationship. For grown children of older adult alcoholics, balance is something they have had little experience with; this middle ground looks like "No Man's Land" to them. Adult children of older alcoholics need education, guidance, and a supportive therapy group to facilitate this change. Counselors can also expect that some of the children will have chemical dependency problems of their own.

Adult Children and Aging Issues

When a chemically dependent older person begins to show signs of aging, this problem is heaped on the pile of other problems their children must deal with. In their hearts, adult children may secretly have dreamed that their chemically dependent father or mother would someday become the "ideal Dad" or "ideal Mom" they never had. As they become aware that this will not happen, they may feel angry, rejected, and disappointed. Adult children may have expected that, through their enabling and caretaking, Mom or Dad would straighten out and become the parent they longed for. As the aging process progresses, and the parent becomes debilitated, or possibly dies, they may feel a deep grief and anger over the loss of the ideal parent that will never be.

For adult children, accepting their parent as chemically dependent can be the beginning of a new, more realistic relationship with them. With understanding and acceptance, adult children can decide how involved they want to be with their parent, and how much emotional distance, love, and respect they need. Sometimes, adult children remain involved only out of a sense of duty. Anytime during the intervention, treatment, or aftercare process, adult children would benefit from their own therapy to help them understand the effect chemical dependency has had on them, what their present wants and needs are, and decide what kind of relationship they want with the dependent parent.

The task of taking care of Mom or Dad is another important, aging issue for adult children. Adult children are often the "in between" person, caring for their parents' needs and the needs of their own children. Adult children often have a job, a spouse, and children. With the responsibilities of these roles, it may be emotionally and financially draining to also care for parents.

A family history of chemical dependency erodes the ability and willingness of adult children to respond to the needs of their parents. Sometimes, the healthiest action for an adult child is to stay away. Perhaps an adult child has uncontrollable anger or becomes overly caretaking when around the dependent parent. Or, perhaps a history of child abuse stands in the way of a child acting to assist a parent. A counselor can help adult children evaluate their situation and discuss alternatives.

Adult children frequently say: "I can't tell my parent what to do." If an adult child still demands that their aging parent fill a parenting role, then the adult child may become stuck in the child role. Other adult children have strong opinions and tend to feel comfortable demanding that their parent take this or that action. Resolving the conflict between their demands, and the reality of their parent's addiction, often requires a counselor's help.

When adult children assume responsibility for their parents, they may mourn the loss of the old relationship between their parent and themselves. They may feel angry, resistant, put upon, or deny that they need to do anything different. When they understand their own resistance to change, they will be able to mature in their relationship with their parents. For adult children in this situation, it is helpful for counselor's to discuss this and encourage them to seek support. Parents and children often need a model of what a healthy parent/child relationship is. Forming this relationship normally starts in later adolescence. In the chemically dependent family, the negotiation needed to form this relationship may never have been done. Perhaps, the adult child never learned to relate to the parent in an adult manner.

If the parent suddenly becomes incoherent from alcohol dementia, a stroke, or another debilitating illness, adult children usually feel loss and grief, or relief and anger. If, however, the aged parent suffers a gradual mental decline, it may be difficult for the family to understand the slow change from impairment due to alcohol abuse to permanent damage. In such a case, the medical consequences of alcoholism need to be dealt with first and family members will need education and help dealing with this problem.

If the chemically dependent parent dies, the family will again need to grieve. They may have felt *anticipatory grief* as the parent became disabled or was placed in a nursing home. The death of the person may bring feelings of relief and resolution. At this time, adult children also become aware that the older generation is no longer a buffer between them and death. This heightened awareness of their own mortality can compound their bereavement and feelings of vulnerability.

SUGGESTIONS FOR COUNSELING CHEMICALLY DEPENDENT OLDER ADULTS AND THEIR FAMILY MEMBERS

So far, I have emphasized the importance of recognizing the uniqueness of each older adult and family. I want to emphasize this again. If counselors are to be effective, it is crucial for them to understand and accept each family member as they are. Counselors must let their patients teach them about themselves. It is equally important for the family to feel understanding and acceptance. Understanding is more than being aware of information gained through test results, it means knowing how it feels to be in that person's shoes. Counselors may not have had the same experiences as their patients, but they can empathize with their feelings and with what their experiences have meant to them. Counselors can try to understand what it feels like to be old and in crisis. Listening is the best way to show understanding.

From this deeper knowing, counselors can give a family total acceptance and touch their humanness. Counselors can help them speak the feelings they are unable to speak. Counselors communicate their understanding and acceptance by saying things such as, "I can imagine what it must have been like for you," and "Even though you were not able to make life happen according to your dreams, I know that you always did the very best you possibly could," or "I understand your hurt and pain."

Counselors gain a family's trust when they listen and try to understand how it was for them. Communicating a judgmental attitude to older adults and families can alienate them and destroy a counselor's effectiveness. Members of alcoholic families are sensitive to judgment; it can trigger their shame. By judging them, counselors only add to their guilt and shame. Counselors must remember the edict: *Do no harm!* Blaming, accusing, shaming, punishing, and labeling are all harmful to these vulnerable individuals.

Counselors must clear up their own issues about their parents, especially if one or both are chemically dependent. Counselors will also benefit from an understanding of their own coping styles, which will make them aware of emotional "hooks" they are susceptible to when counseling older adults and their families. As helping professionals, they also need to discover how they feel about older people and aging. If a counselor is new to working with older adults, they are vulnerable to certain feelings that may trigger intense emotions, but, if a counselor is aware of what triggers these emotions, working with older adults can be an opportunity to continue their growth.

When an addicted older adult enters treatment, he or she may try to induce guilt feelings in the family. They may say, "How can you be so mean?" or "Drinking is not my problem, you're my problem." Or, the family member may direct anger toward the treatment staff, and say *they* are the reason he or she wants to leave treatment. It is important that the staff take direct and immediate action to counteract these behaviors. Family meetings and open discussion of these behaviors is helpful. At this point, it is also important to remember that harsh confrontations or punitive actions could sabotage treatment. The staff and family need to understand that these behaviors are efforts to cope with what the older adult perceives as a threatening or humiliating situation. Family members are helped by hearing that this behavior is common, and if they do not give in to the drinker and take him home, the treatment will probably work.

For many family members, the initial phase of treatment is fearful. Taking time to hear about their fears is especially important for the spouse of the older person. Telling them stories of other families who have successfully gone through treatment is reassuring, and can break through the fear, isolation, and feelings of uniqueness.

If a family member has been a long-time caretaker, she or he may fear that the patient will not receive proper care. One daughter was very upset because her mother, who was in treatment, was not getting a medication she needed. According to her, the nursing staff was not getting it straightened out soon enough, and the staff became angered by the daughter's interference. A major battle was brewing. At a meeting with the counselor, the daughter told of her mother's medical problems and need for certain medications. The head nurse was called into the meeting so that she could listen to the daughter's concerns. They agreed on a plan to deal with the medication. This helped the daughter.

After the nurse left, the counselor continued to listen to the daughter's concerns. Since treatment began, she had visited her mother every day. Clearly, she was very attached to her mother. The counselor validated her concerns by telling her that the staff needed her knowledge of her mother's needs because she knew her mother better than the staff did. The counselor also identified with her about how much of a burden it must have been for her to have been her mother's sole caretaker. Over time, the staff discussed with her how often she needed to visit to feel good that her mother was receiving proper care. Gradually, she relaxed and reduced her visits to twice a week.

It took the family counselor's and the head nurse's explanation at a treatment team meeting to help the rest of the staff change their attitude about this intense daughter. Staff began listening to her and taking time to explain procedures. Eventually, the problem was resolved.

Working with older adults takes time and patience: time to sit and listen; time to establish rapport; time for the family to understand new thinking and to develop new coping skills; time to change old beliefs and ways of behaving; time to adjust to new situations; and time to integrate new knowledge.

Divorce and Separation

Divorce or separation is always a painful decision for the spouse of an older alcoholic. They were taught to believe that marriage is "Till death do us part." For some, divorce is not even an option due to religious beliefs or family tradition. New behaviors, such as refusing to clean up a drinking spouses' mess, calling the police, or even talking with a friend about problems, may feel uncomfortable to the older spouse. Counselors must not use coercion or shame to get them to try new behaviors. Instead, they can expose them to many options, then give them support while they develop their own solutions.

Doris and John's Story

> Doris is sixty-five. John, her husband, had been verbally abusive, even after having gone through chemical dependency treatment four times. She is a devout Catholic and would not consider divorce, even though her children encouraged her to do so. When John was in treatment for the fourth time, she discussed her situation with a counselor who validated her decision not to seek a divorce. Then, they considered how she could have a pleasant and worthwhile life for herself and still stay married to John. She joined an Al-Anon group at her church and became more socially active. In short, she became more independent of John. Be-

cause his behavior did not change after treatment, she and the counselor agreed that John should live in a halfway house. John still has a key to their home, and he comes home frequently. He continues his disturbing behavior, but is no longer a part of her daily life. Doris occasionally invites John home for dinner and continues the marital relationship, but she feels much more control over her own life now. This was her solution, and she was able to make it work.

Abstinence

The therapeutic goal for chemically dependent older adults is always abstinence, but the realities may differ. Minimizing the frequency and quantity of drinking may be a practical solution for some. Regardless of whether abstinence is achieved, the family needs to remember that the chemical abuse is an addiction, and that the addicted family member is not a bad person. The counselor needs to reaffirm to them that addiction is a disease, like chronic diabetes or cancer, and it can recur.

Achieving abstinence may take months, years, or may never occur. Family members will need to discuss how they feel about living with an older adult's addiction. Al-Anon and ACOA participation is often helpful for family members, who often have many issues to deal with that are typical of adult children of alcoholics. The family can learn, with help from a counselor, healthy ways to intervene in an older adult's behavior. If the older adult refuses to allow family intervention or receive help, then family members need to be further encouraged to take care of themselves. Sometimes, even after family treatment, family members give up on the drinker, feeling that they have done everything they could.

Family members of chemically dependent older adults should be encouraged to investigate support resources for themselves, but they should be cautioned that not all people in Al-Anon or ACOA groups will understand what it is like to care about an older adult alcoholic. Some of the advice they will receive may not be appropriate or applicable to their situation. For example, some behaviors described as enabling may be essential for the cognitively or physically impaired older person.

Special Considerations

Counselors must be trustworthy and able to deal with their own feelings about older adults. If a counselor does not get along well with older adults, he or she should investigate that feeling, educate themselves about older adults, and, as a last recourse, consider working with a different group of people. Respect, of course, is vital when providing services to all people, but it is especially critical for older adults. Counselors must watch their attitudes and be willing to explore them and get help if they feel dragged down.

Educating family members about alcoholism, aging, and how they interact is crucial for effective treatment. Special emphasis should be placed on issues of brain damage, other medical complications, and cultural and generational barriers to treatment. It is important to give family members time to absorb new information. Facts about the medical and psychological condition of the chemically dependent older adults will guide the family members in making healthy decisions for themselves and their parent or spouse.

Loss and grief are important issues for families of older adults to deal with. Shame is also an important issue, and staff must be watchful because many things can trigger shame.

Spouses *can* change and that change does not need to be great; sometimes a slight adjustment is enough. Older people are not fragile. Counselors must also recognize that some things will not change, and maybe that is okay for some people.

Some family members may refuse support. Counselors may need to find alternative support for these family members, such as church groups, hobbies, and volunteer opportunities.

Counselors also need to remember that their guidance, if it is not accepted right away, may be accepted in the future.

Counselors must always take care of themselves and their needs. Otherwise they will not be effective with their patients. They need to deal with their own family issues, their own anger and enabling behaviors. They also need a healthy balance–between work, family, and personal time–in their lives. Working with older adults and their families is a rewarding experience and can help counselors prepare for their own aging and plan how they want to live as they age.

INDEX